SECRETS
OF **YOUR CHILD's**
EDUCATION

HIDDEN CAUSES
OF SUCCESS OR FAILURE

ALEXA STUART FRISBIE

CREATOR OF WORKSHOP EDUCATION

Mediacs

New Paltz, New York

Mediacs
151 State Route 32 S #14
New Paltz, New York 12561
mediacs.com

Secrets of Your Child's Education / Alexa Stuart Frisbie

ISBN 978-1-7358460-1-9

Also available as a digital e-book

Dedicated to my talking-time buddy, the first reader of this book, and my sweet pea since age 18, Rick Frisbie. And to our son, Drake, the best gift I have ever received in life.

TABLE OF CONTENTS

IN THE BEGINNING

I hear screaming.

It is coming from my younger brother, a tassel of blond hair framing a furious face. Frustrated about school. Again.

My brother hated going to school. He was an energetic, curious boy who never met a real-life challenge he wouldn't strive to meet.

But he was expected to sit silently all day, listening to other students read haltingly from textbooks. After round robin reading, he answered the even numbered questions in the text. For homework, he answered the odd numbered questions.

Even at lunch, he was expected to be quiet, hushed by claps and yelling from the lunch monitor, amidst the Sloppy Joes. He later recalled feeling like he was literally going to crawl out of his skin. He said he felt like a failure every day of school.

I know what he was expected to do because we went to the same school. I was expected to do the same. The same routine, day after day, year after year, for eight years. My brother suffered. I did too.

I recall staring at the black hand of the huge clock on the wall, watching each minute "thunk" by. I remember the minutes going by so slowly, I had to bite my lip not to cry. I could sit still. My brother could not. This meant trip after trip to the principal's office, for talking or acting out. This meant phone calls from the school and loud arguments at home.

Since our elementary school ended in the 8th grade, I went to a different high school. It was as if I had been living in black and white, and moved to technicolor.

In one history class, we were told we had to teach a part of the content to the rest of the class, using drawings, games or discussions. The teachers often asked us: "Why do you think it is this way? What are your theories?" We were given challenging questions to discuss.

I was so excited, my cheeks were flush. I learned a thousand times more in those four years than I had in the previous eight. This was how different learning could be?

Two thoughts occurred to me during my happy learning years in high school: children are almost entirely captive to the choices adults make regarding their education and because of this, I wanted to help as many children as possible feel good while learning by becoming an educator.

I entered a five-year BA/Master of Teaching program at the University of Virginia. One day, while listening to my education professor lecture about "how lecturing was not a good way to teach," I got the idea for what has become this book.

I pictured a child sitting down to learn, and then pictured what had gone on in the background to impact that experience: unions, publishing companies, research organizations, testing companies, and of course, schools themselves.

I thought, what if one person got a glimpse inside these education institutions, to try to figure out why the system works the way it does — and what can make it better?

I decided to work for two years at each of the following places: a textbook publishing company, public school, private school, testing company, education research organization, and an education union.

I plotted it out, graduated and launched my research project. It didn't go exactly as I had planned.

I worked at education publishing companies, private and public schools, and as a consultant training teachers, but I did not work at a testing company, although a software curriculum job involved preparing students for standardized tests. As an educational researcher though, I did conduct research while completing my master's program. Nor was I employed by an educational union, though I certainly became aware of the unions' impact on the schools in which I taught.

The daily experience of striving to create great educational experiences for hundreds of students helped me further understand what worked and what didn't work for children in the classroom. And that knowledge led to my starting a company offering after-school enrichment classes to thousands of students over the years.

The following note from a former 5th grade student motivated me to write about what I learned during my career-long research project.

"I just want to say that I am very thankful for the experience that I had in [your classroom] and feel that it was easily one of the most positive experiences of my compulsory schooling experience. I can easily say that 5th grade was probably the only grade that I thoroughly enjoyed and thrived within an educational setting during the K-12 years."

How could this happen? Why was only one year in 13 a positive learning experience for this bright, talented boy? What was it about his education that so negatively impacted his learning experience? What could have been done to make it better?

Let's start at the beginning: the first day of school.

Your child's eyes leave your face, and turn to look at the teacher with the question: "Who am I?"

And the teacher begins to tell him or her. They tell children whether they fit, how people should be judged, whether they are okay, and whether they are successes or failures.

Our son's high school teacher told us that when she was young, she thought of herself as a sad child. But then she changed schools and realized she wasn't sad at all. She just hated her hushed school environment, where students were constantly scolded. Moving to a school where she was allowed to talk about what she was thinking, and to interact with the other children, made all the difference.

Schools literally give your child a sense of self.

If a school or a teacher fails a child, the child will blame himself. Just as young children almost automatically see parents fighting as their fault, young children interpret failings on the part of education as their failures.

So how do you help your child thrive while learning?

When you google "help your child get a good education," the same suggestions come up — support reading at home, support the teacher, and create a quiet consistent homework environment.

All of these ideas are helpful to your child's success.

However, there is more to know and consider.

Your decisions — about what school to send your child to, what to do at home, what to comment on, how to interact with that school, what to appreciate in your child's work and classroom — will make a tremendous difference to your child's long-term success, happiness and well-being.

To really help your child get a good education, you need to know the answer to this question: Is the school giving my child the basic things s/he needs to learn and be happy?

For many parents, looking at schools is like me looking at a manual for our TV remote. I am not really quite sure what I am looking at or what to do with it.

After observing hundreds of students learning, day in and day out, I have come to see that children need three basic things to feel happy and successful in their learning. I call them the Three C's — Caring, Connected Curriculum, and Creative Problem Solving. The biggest successes and failures that I have seen correlate almost perfectly to the abundance or lack of three key ingredients.

Children need these three "C's" to thrive in school, and they need them in equal measure.

The real focus of this book is an insider look at what causes them to be lacking. I call them secrets, because without spending time inside schools, publishing houses and the like, I would not have immediately noticed the direct or very indirect impact that certain adult decisions have on children's experience with their learning. They were once secret to me, uncovered by noticing and asking why continuously.

Complex problems have many contributing factors, and this book deep dives into each of these. It isn't a matter of what caused the problem, but how, taken together, institutions and mindsets can accidentally fail to put children's needs first.

I propose solutions for each potential cause of trouble for your child, and try to keep them practical and realistic.

Each of you will notice other causes of less than stellar experiences for your child, and this book provides a model in Part 3 to help you create solutions.

1. What do each of these three "C's" look like behind the scenes?

2. Why do they matter so much to your child?

3. What factors cause them to be missing in some classrooms?

4. How can you hurdle these obstacles on behalf of your child?

Let's start with the first "C" — **Caring**. The range of caring was the first thing I noticed starting off as a young teacher — literally on day one. It was a rough wake up call.

PART I
THE FIRST "C"
—CARING—

WHAT I HAVE SEEN

Warning: this part of the book will be hardest to read and to take in. It certainly has been for me. Please note that most teachers are kind, so breathe easy. But for the sake of your child, and being aware, open your mind to the possibility that not all will be, and your child will need your support in that case.

Starting my Master of Teaching program, I was impressed that the program immediately put us into classrooms observing or teaching. But what I loved about the program almost immediately became something I hated.

A few days into my first assignment, the teacher I was working with screamed at an overwhelmed first grader. She yelled at him to go clean up the bookshelf where a few books had fallen on the floor. So, he headed over to the shelf to clean it up, looking rattled.

Then the teacher almost immediately screamed at him again, this time because he wasn't lined up with the rest of the class to go to lunch. She had screamed at him to do two different things, at once. He couldn't please her, and she was scaring him. And when I say screamed, I am not exaggerating. She screamed!

The first grader stood paralyzed, his blue eyes filling with tears, holding the books in his hand that he was desperately trying to get back onto the shelf. She didn't seem to care at all that he was welling up. She screamed at him more.

A semester later, I was placed with a brilliant instructor. The children glowed when she was around. She asked what they thought. What I thought. She always took the time to lean down or kneel on one knee to be at eye level when speaking with children, and taught me to do the same. She smiled lovingly even at children who could not sit still to save their lives. She taught me strategies to calm students, and how to get them through trying transitions. She was nearing retirement age and had maintained a serenity and integrity of thinking that blew me away. The children learned, eager to grow in her kindness.

These two teachers were like night and day.

It didn't surprise me when teachers were nice. I expected that. What did surprise me was that teachers can be mean.

Looking back on these experiences, I shouldn't have been so shocked. This was a pattern I had already seen in my own elementary school. It was so common, so "normal," and such an integral part of the school, that it was invisible to me at the time. Even if you weren't the one being screamed at and humiliated in front of peers, there was an anxiety spike heading into school. What if you were next?

The range of caring your child experiences from year to year can vacillate unpredictably between three types of teachers: teacher-bullies, teacher-deflators, and teacher-champions.

TEACHER-BULLIES

One lunch period, I was waiting with my class to go into the cafeteria for lunch. A teacher came up behind one of my most shy and sweet 5th grade boys and, without warning, grabbed the baseball cap off of his head and began screaming at him that hats were not allowed.

This was not a school rule, and I allowed my students to wear baseball caps, since the sun could be blinding on the treeless blacktop area during recess after lunch.

I saw the boy's eyes well up. He asked me quietly to go to the bathroom. He didn't want his 5th grade peers to see him cry.

Normally very non-confrontational, I went into the teacher's classroom during that lunch break and told her to never speak to one of my students like that again.

She didn't, at least when I was around, but the damage was done.

My students couldn't even relax in the lunch line.

Another year, I started the first day of school with a class meeting. A boy started talking, and the rest of the class yelled "off topic." "Wait, why are you saying that?" I asked.

"Our second-grade teacher told us to yell that when he gets off topic," they said.

Imagine for a moment, really imagine, how it feels to start talking and hear "off topic" yelled from the rest of the class, year after year, from 2nd to 5th grade. It was a testament to his perseverance that he was even talking at all.

Though obviously angry, once he was allowed to talk, his comments were some of the most insightful I've ever heard in a classroom. He had this wonderful way of connecting something to the topic at hand that at first seemed disparate or "off topic." His classmates came to very much respect him for this talent.

I have typically encountered only one or two teacher-bullies in a school, say out of 30 or so. But when you multiply one or two teachers by how many students they impact year after year after year — they are heavy-weights in the bully culture.

The next category of teachers I have seen repeatedly are teacher-deflators.

TEACHER-DEFLATORS

I once saw a primary grade child put his head down and refuse to do writing homework. I couldn't understand why, because the assignment was to write a simple summary. Then I looked at the previous summary he had written, a well-stated summary of a movie. In response, he got back from the teacher an entire page of negative notes, written in small print. The teacher asked for a summary, but wanted an essay. He was thoroughly confused. He was giving up.

Teacher-deflators provide either a flat response, or a critical one, over and over again. The teacher-deflator fixates on deficits. Even when the critical comments are mild, they just add up.

One year, I was summoned to our after-school enrichment classes because a child seemed overly angry. I noticed that whenever he made a mistake, or even when he did what others were doing, classmates would call out his name, as if he were at fault.

I also noticed the teachers said his name repeatedly in front of the class in a corrective way. While calling out his name seemed innocuous, the children were mimicking the teacher, in a more yelling, critical tone. The result was that the child was constantly being embarrassed by being called out. It is amazing how quickly a class can scapegoat a child if the teacher is not very, very careful.

Once the teachers started talking more privately and quietly with the child, the overall classroom situation improved for the child.

TEACHER-CHAMPIONS

The third and final type of teacher is the teacher-champion. These teachers see the best in children and, by so doing, inspire the children to want to be their best. They see and accept the child for who he or she is — not just a lump of clay that can be molded or crafted, but an individual worthy of the teacher-champion's care and attention.

This caring is the difference between gazing at the tree in your yard and seeing all the beautiful dancing leaves, or just seeing all the dead branches that need to be trimmed.

When you ask teacher-champions about their teaching day, they often break out into a smile and share an anecdote revealing their great empathy for the children they teach. Or a triumph they have worked towards all year.

Teacher-champions aren't generally showy. They are thoughtful and authentic in their comments. If a teacher who finds students annoying oohs and aahs over their work, the students sense the disconnect.

There are other teachers who do care about the children and are quite strict and reserved. Their impact on children can be equally life changing.

In my first textbook editing job, I was taught to follow this formula to get the very best writing from authors:

1. Focus first on the author's writing strengths, in as much detail as possible.

2. Explain why the strengths worked. The author is going to produce better writing by understanding and re-using those strengths.

3. Set goals and be very specific about what they are and how to reach them.

That, in a nutshell, is what good teachers do.

We had a student in our after-school classes who had been told he was too pessimistic. One of our teachers explained to him how this skill could come in handy.

She reframed it like this: You are good at predicting what might go wrong, and you could use this ability to prevent things from going wrong.

When I interviewed engineers while writing science curriculum for NASA, I learned that the primary job of a mission planner is to predict the thousands of things that could go wrong during the mission, and then try to prevent them from occurring or have back-up plans for dealing with each failure. This strong "what could go wrong" trait may drive people crazy in one profession, but can be a huge asset in another.

Our teacher was absolutely correct in noting that pessimism can be a strength in certain situations. She recognized the child's ability, and helped him make the most of it. That's what teacher-champions do.

This teacher created challenges that involved him doing that for various projects. He was recognized by the class for this ability. He beamed.

Teacher-champions have a sense of presence and patience that makes your child feel safe and happy. It is their caring and authentic day-after-day comments that inflate your child.

The wide range of uncaring to caring behaviors I've observed through the years has surprised me more than anything else I have witnessed in education.

How this range of caring behavior, in its many variations, can impact your child's day-to-day schooling is the topic of the next chapter.

WHY IT MATTERS

It seems obvious that the unkind actions described above will be harmful to your child. What more needs to be said?

Well, a bit more… because a teacher's lack of caring or positive caring is amplified by certain factors, and often produce ripple effects on your child that extend far beyond the original event.

If your child is bullied in school by a teacher, your child's self-esteem will plummet quickly, and be difficult to recover. Your child will create a negative inner voice that can be hard to shake. And his or her self-consciousness and anxiety will be amplified to an excruciating degree by the fact that potential friends and classmates are witnessing his being bullied. It is public and embarrassing.

It is important to note something that may not be intuitive: teachers bullies often single out one or two students in a class to bully, while welcoming other children to be in their camp. So, though your child tells you the teacher is nice to them, he still may be witnessing bullying behavior by the teacher towards other classmates.

Another possible, and not uncommon negative impact on your child, is that the experience of watching a teacher bully other children may encourage him or her to become a bully.

A parent told me when their child was targeted and bullied by the teacher, his peers turned on him as well. And not just for that school year. This abusive treatment by his peers continued long after that year ended, and the impact was devastating.

Why does this happen?

When an individual, particularly a young child, witnesses something scary, like a person being bullied, a defense mechanism often kicks in. It goes like this: "The victim did something to deserve it. I won't do that. Therefore, I am safe." The scarier the situation is, the more this emotional survival strategy kicks in.

My father, who was a pilot in WWII, said that each evening, when many of his friends had not returned from the day's mission, the surviving pilots convinced themselves those who didn't survive were poor pilots. Looking back, he said this was, of course, ridiculous. Often the planes simply malfunctioned, and it was a crapshoot who would get shot down. But each day's surviving pilots held tight to the mythology that if you were shot down, it was because you were a poor pilot. Otherwise, my father said, they never would have climbed back into the cockpit the next day.

When bad things happen to others, they did something wrong, it was their fault. But the reality is more like, "There but for the grace of God, go I." Some outcomes are just too scary to fathom, to imagine them happening to you.

Children do the same thing when it comes to bullying. If they believe the child being bullied by a teacher deserves it, in their mind they are safe from similar treatment.

Some children will curry favor with the teacher by telling on the "victim" or even bullying a classmate who is being targeted by the teacher. In this way, they are protecting themselves from being bullied by the teacher.

Thinking about it in this way, it makes sense that your child might be cruel to a classmate bullied by the teacher. Or, if your child feels scared and powerless watching the teacher bully another child, he will randomly bully other children to restore his self-confidence.

Even if your child is not being bullied or bullying, watching other children being bullied in school generates anxiety. School is not a safe place.

My first encounter with a teacher-bully was during my first student teaching experience. The children were quiet, turned in on themselves, preoccupied with the need to avoid the teacher's bullying. They were barely learning.

Year after year of teaching, I saw students who came from the classes of teacher-bullies. Almost all of them were initially quite unkind to each other, defeated, and shell-shocked.

Bullying is the least caring situation your child could experience. Moving up one rung on the caring scale takes us to excessive criticism or scolding, the realm of the teacher deflators. How do these teachers impact your child?

I had an experience as an adult that reminded me of the potential impact of deflators. I am embarrassed to share it because the experience didn't involve criticism or scolding. But it did give me renewed empathy for what it is like to be a student.

Once, in a teacher-writing workshop, I volunteered to share a paragraph I had written. I am only "medium shy" about reading my writing. For the previous pieces shared by others, the teacher-leader thanked the participants and commented on the strengths she noted in their writing.

When I finished reading my paragraph, the teacher-leader didn't say anything. She just stared at me and said, "Anyone else want to share?"

I suddenly wished I had not shared, and just felt . . . not so great.

I am sure she was distracted by the time or was thinking about what she needed to do next. It was one tiny, tiny moment. I was already an adult. I was already confident about my writing in general. Luckily, I had grown up with a mother who listened to my stories and instilled in me an early love of writing. I only share that story to set the stage for one that followed.

I remember a telephone call from a very stressed parent. He called to complain that his kindergartner was not benefiting from our Study Skills enrichment class. We met with the teacher to discuss his complaint.

It turned out that his real concern was that the teacher was not correcting his kindergartener's writing.

Our teacher had focused on encouraging the new writer to connect sounds and letters. The child had learned almost all of the consonants, which was impressive.

The parent pulled out a previous homework assignment by his kindergartener. It looked bloodied. The teacher had scrawled red corrections everywhere, trying to transform a child's first fledging idea that "m" makes the "em" sound into a complex sentence.

I had been puzzled by why this particular school had so many students who didn't like writing, and as a result, whose writing skills were below standard. Students at our other schools loved to write and were quite proficient. Seeing that fledgling sentence, I began to understand the underlying problem.

If I can recall one moment when my writing was received so critically as an adult, then I would realize how this kindergartener must have felt getting his first heavily red-penciled written assignment back.

People sometimes forget that writing, and really much of learning, is in essence a vulnerable activity. You put something out, and how it is received determines how you view yourself. These moments sear in our brain who we are and what we are like as learners. You cannot underestimate their importance.

You may think, "My child just hates writing," without realizing that his problem with writing is linked to negative school experiences.

Being scolded and criticized publicly may not rise to the level of bullying, but it also takes a toll on a child. It may cause anxiety.

When you see a child flinch or slightly withdraw when approached by an adult at school, that is a child who has been overly scolded and criticized.

Your child may be in a "death by a thousand cuts" situation, mentally battered by the impact of repeated criticisms.

Growing up, I had a foreign language teacher who made me stand by my desk while responding to her dialogue prompts. Since I was very shy, the act of standing up by my desk was excruciating.

I would try to respond to her prompts, but as I stood there, exposed, she would become exasperated, and say: "No! Try again." I would try again, and she would once again say: "No! Try again."

By then, I was feeling so embarrassed, I couldn't hear or understand her dialogue prompts.

After what seemed like an eternity, she told me to sit down in a voice dripping with disgust.

To this day, I am not sure what I did wrong.

Unless you know me well, you wouldn't notice the long-term impact of these interactions. I was confident academically, and therefore able to get A's in foreign language classes. But to this day, being asked to speak a foreign language causes me to freeze me up like a deer in headlights. My mind goes blank from fear.

You might argue that maybe I am just awful at speaking foreign languages, and this difficulty has nothing to do with my experience with an impatient teacher. But if that teacher had been encouraging, rather than impatient and exasperated, I might have developed more proficiency in speaking a foreign language.

The anxiety of being embarrassed and exposed in the classroom by a critical teacher can turn off a child's learning curve, perhaps for a lifetime.

Anxiety impairs learning. Our threat response system is incredibly powerful. When that threat system is activated in the core of our brain, the brain shuts down the prefrontal cortex in order to focus on the need to fight or flee. Unfortunately, the prefrontal cortex is where reasoning and learning happens. So, if your child feels unsafe in school, his prefrontal cortex will shut down and his learning will be negatively impacted.

Anxious children taught by unkind teachers may associate the class subject with negative feelings. Without positive intervention to dispel their negative connotations, they could avoid and dislike that subject for many years, if not a lifetime.

When I ask adults about the origin of their dislike for a subject area, they almost always cite an interaction with a teacher-bully or -deflator.

That is not what you want for your child.

As my father once said regarding his service in WWII, it is easier to know what you are fighting against — Nazism — than to know what you are fighting for.

So, here is what parents should fight for: Teacher-champions. But who are teacher-champions, and what makes them worth fighting for?

Children flourish when they are liked. Not because they do what the teacher wants, but because the teacher finds something quite lovable in them, even when they are twirling around in the back of the room when the teacher is reading a story. It is easy to love children when they behave. But when a child is treated kindly even when he doesn't fall in line, he feels truly loved.

A teacher's deep, unconditional caring builds a sense of safety that will free your child's brain to learn, and the child will try hard to hurdle all performance goals.

A caring teacher is genuinely curious to hear what the child thinks. In conversation with the child, the teacher will come to understand the child's unique traits, and how they can be used to best advantage in his or her education.

A caring teacher will know that verbally and physically impulsive children will do well in situations that require taking risks and not overthinking things.

The caring teacher will see that a child who is a terrible follower may be a great leader. You might not even recognize the child as the same person when you put them in charge of something.

A caring teacher will help your child love school and learning. Whenever a person says they love a topic, ask when they first encountered the topic. Whether it be a kind adult showing them bugs in the backyard or a teacher who connects with them over history, the personal relationship almost always proceeds the interest in the topic.

There is nothing more important for your child's educational experience than a caring teacher. The positive impact of caring is profound, and the negative impact can be very damaging.

Since caring is so fundamental to the entire learning experience, we should be able to say this: Children and adults should be able to expect consistency of caring in each year of school. So why is this not the case?

---◇---

CAUSES & FIXES

Given that caring is so important, why might this be difficult to get for your child?

Why is there a range of caring from bully to deflator to champion?

Let's start with some of the hidden causes that can fan the flames for caring failures, followed by what you can try in order to hurdle these obstacles for your child.

CAUSE 1
ASSUMING ALL TEACHERS ARE NICE

In primary school, our son said this repeatedly about his teacher: "She is mean."

Me: "She is just strict. Just really try extra hard to behave in her class."

I made one big assumption.

My son had been happy the year before. He was bright, testing in the 99th percentile. He loved to write stories for fun. Within a month of this new grade with the "mean" teacher, he decided he was terrible at everything, bit the skin off his fingers, and said he wished he were dead because "life is school." We tried hard to figure out why he was devolving.

We looked carefully at:

- our home life
- his learning needs (we did an expensive round of testing)
- friendships
- possible medical concerns

I enlisted the teacher's help in finding out why my son's self-esteem had plummeted so dramatically. She couldn't think of any reason. Nor could we.

At the end of the year, a parent told us he had seen the teacher ripping up our son's paper, and screaming in his face, "Why can't you ever do anything right?"

When I asked our son about this, he said that his teacher did that all the time. "I told you she was mean," he said.

I thought "mean" meant strict. I was wrong. "Mean" meant mean.

For years afterwards, our son would rip up writing assignments, rather than turn them in. It wasn't until his sophomore year of high school, when a teacher recommended his short story for an award, that he begin to discard the idea that he was a terrible writer.

Mean teachers can do lingering damage to children. But in this case, I share part of the blame for my son's plummeting self-esteem.

Why didn't I hear my child when he told me his teacher was mean? Why do other parents make this same mistake? Here are some of the reasons:

- I didn't want to think or accept that my child wouldn't be safe in his classroom. It was beyond what I ever imagined would be true, even though I had encountered mean teachers as a child and as a teacher.
- I assumed the teacher's meanness was based on his misbehavior in the classroom, that the teacher was strict. It was just simpler to tell him to behave.

Somehow, I was unable to believe that the teacher-bullies I had experienced as a pupil and observed as a teacher would inflict their meanness on my child.

Some part of me may have normalized the way some teacher-bullies abuse children, and therefore not seen it for what it was. This is very hard for me to admit.

A friend told me when growing up, she was tied to a tree and basically tortured by her "girlfriends." When she tried to tell her mom, her mom said, "Just ignore it or you'll make it worse."

The daughter was trying to tell her mother she was being bullied. But the mother was hearing something else, something less terrible.

Today's generation of parents now see child bullying as a serious matter, and not just "part of being a kid."

Parents often view whatever experience they had growing up as normal or the standard. They expect their children will share the same experiences they did. If some of their teachers screamed at them, that's the norm their children will experience.

In short, many parents turn a blind eye to abusive teacher behavior, even when it's directed towards young children, simply because it happened to them when they were kids. It is just part of school.

If a child rips up the paper of another child and says, "you can't do anything right," the behavior would be seen as abusive and corrected. But when a teacher does the same thing, it usually goes unnoticed.

Since adults don't have a word to accurately describe the behavior of teacher-bullies, children don't have the vocabulary to communicate what is happening to them. So, they will use the word "mean," which is widely interpreted by parents as "strict." And their complaint is dismissed.

Here are ways to prevent this misunderstanding, and help your child if he or she is being abused by a teacher-bully:

FIX 1
If Your Child is Struggling, Consider the Teacher Along with Other Possibilities

When our son's behavior changed and his self-esteem plummeted, I considered a ton of possible reasons. But I overlooked what had immediately precipitated the change — a new grade and a new teacher. When you notice a change in your child, turn over every stone for the cause, and consider the child's teacher and classroom as well.

FIX 2
Examine Your Expectations for the Level of Caring from Teachers

You are probably aware of the need to reflect on the impact of your parents on your own parenting. Without this reflection, people often blindly repeat parenting behaviors — even behavior they hated as children — instead of considering a broader array of choices to see what might be best.

This same type of reflection about your schooling is useful. Here are some examples drawn from my own school experience, which I hope will stimulate your own reflection. Jot down your thoughts on the two questions. Ask other family members the same questions:

What was one of your best experiences with a teacher growing up? Why did you like it?

My English teacher in high school paid a lot of attention to my writing. She said she saw a lot of potential in me, which made me open to her suggestions. She gave me lots of feedback, and the strengths were well balanced with goals.

She wasn't overly controlling, and kind of let me accept which feedback to use in my edits. For example, she often wrote "too conversational" on my papers, but I really felt being conversational was more fun to read, so we kind of joked back and forth about it.

What was one of your worst experiences with a teacher growing up? Why did you not like it?

I will count my foreign language teacher's routines as being up there, though I don't consider it bullying, as she made everyone stand up to answer. It just wasn't a good match for how my mind was working and how shy I was.

But "normalizing poor behavior" doesn't completely explain my misunderstanding of what my son was telling me about his teacher's abusive behavior. Why else would I so misconstrue the level of caring my child was getting in school?

CAUSE 2
ALWAYS BACKING THE TEACHER

There is another notion that I acquired while growing up that may explain why I misconstrued my child's complaint. My parents' motto was to always back the teacher — a good idea, if the teacher is trustworthy.

If they are not trustworthy, this blind trust can be damaging to your child because he or she will follow your lead and trust them blindly, too.

If your child doesn't know that adults can be untrustworthy, they are at a distinct disadvantage when encountering someone who doesn't deserve their trust.

Many adults fear ruining their child's innocence with even the idea they cannot trust those around them, particularly adults. The younger the child, the more the parents want to preserve the idea that the world is a completely safe place and everyone can be trusted.

However, this idea can indirectly contribute to the problem of children not getting the caring they need, because the child internalizes the actions of an untrustworthy adult as their fault. The child who believes all adults are trustworthy will process a teacher's unkind behavior as justified and deserved. Adults can do no wrong. Therefore, your child may not tell you about an unkind or noncaring teacher.

In addition, recipients of unkindness, both children and adults, often try to feel more in control of an out-of-control situation by thinking the unkind behavior could have been prevented had they done something different. Parents and children can both do this.

Think back to an experience of being treated poorly. Does the memory make you feel ashamed? Did you do anything wrong to deserve the bad treatment? Parents who were shamed by the bad treatment of others are more likely to pass this along to their children.

For example, take my experience with the foreign language teacher. Today, many years later, I now understand that making me stand up in class and yelling at me was a super ineffective teacher strategy. But for years after that embarrassing experience, I felt it was my fault for being "bad" at foreign language.

Parents sometimes assume their children are being bullied by the teacher or other children because they did something wrong. "What did you do?" they might ask the child. This misunderstanding, which might reflect their own childhood experience of blaming themselves for being bullied, can be very damaging to a child.

How can you, the parent, prevent your child from the self-blame of being bullied?

FIX 1
Teach Concept of Trustworthiness

Teach your child that people gain or lose trust by their behavior. Trust is something each adult must earn. And you can trust someone for one thing, but not for another. Give you child examples of who has gained your trust and why. For example, you may trust a friend to be supportive when you are going through a hard time, but not to remember to drop something off for you, because they are absent-minded.

Follow up these conversations with discussions about what makes a teacher trustworthy, what a teacher should do to meet the criteria for trustworthiness.

These discussions should provide your child with a clear sense of the following:

- Teachers should be kind to students.

- Teachers should make learning interesting.

- Teachers should try to work with the class to make things better.

This will give your child the idea that, while most people are trustworthy, not all people are. That if people and teachers act in a caring and kind way, they gain your trust. If they don't, they don't gain it. Trust is yours to give after evaluation, not a given.

Beyond this general concept, keep reinforcing what caring and non-caring behaviors look like to your child and those around you, and what your child deserves.

FIX 2
Thank Caring Teachers

If your child shares kind things a teacher has done, you might want to suggest your child write a thank you note, or bring a flower into class, or do something kind in return to say thanks. Keep on asking your child about what they liked about that day in class or the teacher's behavior. This will help your child develop an understanding of what makes a good relationship.

You should also support caring behavior by thanking the teacher in person or in writing. Describe specifically what you like about her teaching, the positive impact her caring is having on your child. Share your comments with the school's administrators, such as the curriculum director, vice principal, principal, or team leader.

You want administrators to know how much this caring teaching means to your child, so they continue to emphasize the importance of caring as the basis for a positive learning relationship.

Doing this also helps administrators see things in a teacher they may otherwise miss. A teacher once drew an amazing portrait of each child when they were the star of the week. The portrait was sent home with the child. If parents had not informed the school's administrations about the portraits, the principal would never have known about the many hours the teacher devoted to this on her own time.

Thanking teachers for their caring behavior and informing school administrators will make the teacher feel rewarded and make the school better.

FIX 3
Frame Your Child's Understanding of
How They Should be Treated

If your child tells you the teacher has acted unkindly, immediately help your child frame what he or she is experiencing and discard any inaccurate assumptions learned by the child. If the child made a mistake, say disrupted a lesson, you can help the child understand that, while it was not a great idea to disrupt a lesson, the teacher should never respond in such an unkind manner.

Give your child the opportunity to share their feelings. Just listen.

And, then, give your child your perspective by telling him or her that all children might make the same mistake (whatever led to the unkind treatment). One example would be forgetting to write your name on a school paper, and having the teacher rip up the paper. Learning to write your name on the paper is a very normal part of learning, but there are kind ways to teach it. Explain that good teachers help students learn things like this without doing mean things.

You want the child to understand that, while putting the name on a paper is a smart thing to do, tearing up a paper or yelling is not okay. You want to get the message across that your child did not deserve to be treated unkindly. The Cliff Notes version that your child needs to hear is this:

- Children will make mistakes.

- Teachers will feel frustrated or angry at times.

- Both of these are okay and normal.

- Being abusive or mean to a child is not okay.

No one deserves this treatment, no matter what the reason.

Your child needs to hear this, immediately and unequivocally, before you focus your attention on the teacher or school.

The fact your child knows you don't approve of the teacher's unkind treatment is huge. It will make a big difference in how much they internalize what happens and what is said.

We all encounter authority figures who yell and demean, so it's important to help your child develop the strength to see such bad behavior as the other person's problem, rather than their fault. Mentally protecting yourself from an unkind person is something we all need to learn. By helping your child accurately frame an unkind teacher's behavior, you are making the most of a bad situation, while at the same time passing on a valuable life skill to your child.

You can tell your child you will come up with a plan to make it stop (addressed a bit later in the book), but for now, you can leave it at that, and give yourself time to think.

So far, you have communicated how you feel about what your child has shared, and have given them another perspective to counter their assumption that "I must be a bad kid. I got yelled at for not putting a name on the paper."

Sadly, there is yet another reason that some teachers get away with treating students poorly — blind obedience.

CAUSE 3
VALUING BLIND OBEDIENCE

Most parents want obedience from their children. Adults often respect other parents whose children immediately and quickly obey. And it is easy to see why. Things feel in control and, therefore, easier.

But every asset, if taken to the extreme, is a liability.

If your child never objects or questions your commands, you might be raising someone who blindly obeys out of fear. The problem is they may also be blindly obeying untrustworthy adults or cruel peers.

Parents often tell their children: "Do as I say. Do as I say. Do as I say." And then they send them off into the world with the instruction to "Think for yourself."

As Neil deGrasse Tyson said, "We spend the first year of a child's life teaching it to walk and talk and the rest of its life to shut up and sit down. There's something wrong there."

A child who is beaten down (figuratively) for stating a different point of view in the face of authority is much less likely to tell you when someone is being abusive. How can you protect your child from losing his voice and accepting poor treatment?

FIX 1
Problem Solve with Your Child

The goal is to not to override your child's voice completely, but to incorporate it into problem solving. This equips your child to be able to stick up for themselves when they need to — when you are not there to protect them.

Here is how to give your child a voice:

- Figure out your point of view and what you want (as a parent) and why you want it. (Hold this in your thoughts for now.)
- Ask questions that will encourage your child to reveal his point of view.
- Acknowledge your child's point of view.
- Share your point of view.
- Work together to come up with solutions that take into account both your and your child's point of view. Test them, and then circle back.

A shorthand way to remember this is to seek first to understand and then be understood, and then come up with solutions that can work for both. The trick here is balance.

Some parents talk in circles endlessly with their children, asking what they want. The parents seem to erase themselves from the equation, and it can be painful to watch and unhealthy for the child.

On the other end of the spectrum, there are the parents who overpower children. They could care less what the child is thinking or feeling, as long as they are complying. The healthy place is in the middle — both sides learn to communicate, and both sides become creative problem solvers.

Teaching these important skills sets the stage for better treatment for your child, at school and in life.

But what happens when you have trained your child to see right from wrong, and they see wrong from an authority figure? Then you have a different set of issues to deal with.

CAUSE 4
BEING BLINDED BY FEAR OF PAYBACK

We have all seen movies where someone stands up to someone in power and it ends well. In real life, however, we have also seen the very real repercussions of confronting someone who has more power than we do.

One year, my husband recalls, his 6th grade teacher rarely showed up to teach, sending in subs with no sub plan. When she did come to school, she had a designated student show back to back movies, while she smoked in the teacher's lounge. My husband did not share this information with his mother. However, his mom noticed there were no reading assignments that year, or any real homework. So, unbeknownst to my husband, his mom wrote a nicely phrased note to his 6th grade teacher, suggesting that they could have books to read, and writing to do.

The next day, after receiving the note, the teacher did come in. For the whole school day, she made the students take turns reading slowly from the dictionary. The rest of the class had to copy each word and definition. Recess was canceled and so was PE. When a student asked why they had to do this, the teacher said that Rickie's mom had put a note in her box that the students should do more reading and writing. My husband was not very popular with his peers that day.

Sometimes parents do learn that a teacher is saying mean things to their child, and are rightfully upset. However, they often respond with statements like this: If I complain, it will just make it worse for her. It turns out that teacher is responsible for picking the volleyball team, so we just have to put up with it.

If a parent complains, they are still typically sending the child into that classroom each day, with added ire from the teacher. This can lead adults to look away from a situation that they don't know how to impact.

One important thing to remember for your young learner is that "those in power" aren't just movie producers, CEO's and politicians. For a child, a parent volunteer coaching soccer is someone in power. Just wait until your child gets cut from the team or doesn't get playing time. In fact, if you think about it, really everyone in your child's life has way more power than your child does. This fear can immobilize parents — for good reason — as payback does exist when you question the wrong person. How can you overcome this hurdle and help your child?

FIX 1
Teach Strategies for Managing Payback Potential

As children get older, you want to engage them in thinking about when and how you stand up to those in power, especially if issues of right and wrong are involved.

If you know something is wrong, and confronting it involves confronting someone with power to damage you, the realistic options are these:

- You may decide it isn't worth the fight, or that payback is not manageable at that particular time.
- You may decide it is worth questioning, but only to a certain degree.

- You may decide it is totally worth questioning, but plan ahead to try to put yourself in the position to avoid the punishment that may await. For example, you may want others to join with you, reducing the likelihood the person in authority can retaliate. Or, find one key person, who is also in power, to back you.

For example, in college, a professor said she wouldn't pass my master's thesis because, during a brief weekly check-in she had scheduled in the evening, I was waitressing. She didn't seem to understand how much I needed the money to stay in school, and asked if my parents knew what my priorities were. They did.

I wasn't very strategic at the time and had no idea what to do about my thesis. But it just so happened, right after I heard the news, that I found myself in the elevator with the Dean of the Education School. He asked how I was, and I said I was not very good. We talked, and I explained the situation. He asked to read my thesis, gave it an A, and submitted it to Education Resources Information Center (ERIC) where it was accepted and published. That was good luck. More training to advocate for myself would have led me to seek him out, rather than just bumping into him.

As your children get older, share stories of when you or others questioned authority. In the story, share the reality – the morality of it, and the potential backlash. Decipher for them the ways in which people made themselves safer and more effective.

I promise, even having some insight into this thought process is a life skill, which will help your children tremendously. Or by starting this conversation, you may become the person they turn to when facing these types of dilemmas. They may reach out for your counsel, rather than just turning a blind eye, and feeling compromised as a result.

Next let's examine three words, that you think would help, but that can separate you from understanding what is going on in your child's classroom.

CAUSE 5
FAILING TO COMMUNICATE

How many times have you had this exchange?

Parent: "How was school?"

Child (looking annoyed or tired): "Fine."

It's not telling you much. But by repeating it, we can feel like we asked. We did the best we could, and we can leave it at that. But if you get no information, there has to be a better way. What to do instead?

FIX 1
Have Regular Talking Time

One of the best pieces of advice I got when our son was a baby was to set up a routine for talking time, when you don't really have an agenda. Before bed, although the parent is tired, is actually a great time. Because if it is between going to sleep or keeping a conversation going, children will often choose talking — when they might not otherwise. Starting this routine is a safeguard, because you will have set the stage for them to be open with you if they are encountering difficulties. You can start the bedtime a little earlier to make room for this.

FIX 2
Show Empathy

When you discuss schoolwork with your child, lead with empathy. When children feel that you care about them, in addition to the work they are producing, they are much more motivated. There is a simple way to do that. Look at what work they are being assigned, and think about how you would feel doing it at their age. And just start with an empathetic statement, such as, "That looks hard." "Wow, that is a lot of work due in a short time." "It must be hard to be doing this work after a long soccer practice."

This helps the child understand that you get it. You might think this acknowledgment of what they are facing demotivates a child or gives them an out, but I have found the opposite to be true. With empathy, you become a team working together, and your child may start being more open about school experiences in general.

FIX 3
Active Listening — Tell Me More

During this talking time, or whenever it works, as a refrain, periodically ask something about teachers and coaches. Choose an option that feels most natural to you. Share your own stories about these questions to connect with your child.

- Who is (was) your favorite and least favorite teacher/coach? Why?

- Once you get your child talking, use this refrain:
  Tell me more.
  How is she nice?
  How is s/he mean?

Initially, it might be better not to add "to you" at the end, as it can make children embarrassed and ashamed if they are being treated poorly, and they may be less likely to share details with you. It can also make them freeze up remembering it. But if you ask what type of things the person does in general, this can relax the anxiety that the question can provoke.

Try to get more specifics to understand the situation better:

- What exactly? Give an example.

If something is not clear, ask follow up questions to get a clearer picture.

- How loud was she talking? Did she seem mad?

- Listen with genuine curiosity.

Here are other ways to try to learn more about school:

- What types of things get students in trouble at school?
- What types of things do students get away with at school?

The goal is to have a set routine, and ongoing conversations around their experiences at school to learn more.

Now let's leave the mindsets and routines at home that can help or hinder your child's level of caring at school, and venture into the teaching conditions that can impact the level of caring.

CAUSE 6
LOW PAY AND PRESTIGE

My mother, who had been a teacher before leaving to raise six children, had this to say about my choice to pursue my Masters in Teaching, "Why would you do that? You could do anything."

I guess for her it was one of few options. While, for me, she felt I had many options, and thought I could do "better."

I did have many options, but I most cared about helping children feel happy and successful at school. And I felt there was so much work to do in this area.

But to her point (and mothers do often have a point), the prestige and respect from other adults is only there spottily. The external markers of success that most jobs provide are few and far between. In my first job in publishing, I received two promotions and two raises within the first year and a half. As a teacher, you are on tiny pay scale steps. And everyone is on the same steps.

I don't think low pay and prestige are a reason for non-caring teachers. You can look at the plethora of amazing, caring teachers working under the same conditions as other teachers to see that.

However, low pay and prestige are part of the reason there aren't a larger pool of teachers to select from. Many individuals who might love teaching and be amazing, bypass it due to low pay and prestige. And a smaller pool of teachers to choose from can very much impact who will educate your child.

In addition to lack of prestige, teaching can literally hamper your options in life. Though we live in a mobile global work force, the public school system is stuck in feudal times. If you switch school districts, even just one district over, say from San Francisco to Marin, many districts start you back at step one of the pay scale. The beginning pay step is generally horrible, so you are hugely incentivized to stay in the same place. But this can lead to frustration, as you may not be able to make the best decisions for your life or your family.

On top of possibly going back to the beginning pay scale, if you switch states, you also have to go through a cumbersome process of getting re-credentialed in that state. There is little to no logic to the requirements to transfer credentials between states. Virginia had high standards for my credential. I had a Masters. Surely that would work with California children. In my case, and for most teachers, you have to sit out a year to get through a mountain of paperwork and repeat classes. The new state loses out on a possible candidate to choose from that year, even when there are teaching shortages.

At the same time, having had a variety of jobs related to education, I can say that teaching has certainly been the most demanding of all of them.

To be an effective teacher, you have to be enormously energetic, patient, and very smart. You have to create a structure of routines that work, figure out the best way to teach all that you have to teach, and determine ways to give children the feedback they need.

You are literally all in. If you care — then you care about academic success and emotional success. And there are hundreds of things to problem solve about each one. It can be hard to turn it off to regroup.

When you see children in tough situations, it can be hard to sleep at night. At times, what the child might be dealing with — sexual, physical or emotional abuse — can truly break your heart.

You are connected to a larger community. But when there are tragedies, you are impacted deeply. Your heart grows bigger, but it gets broken more.

When you are teaching, there is no taking a phone call to fix your car. There is no sitting for five minutes to digest some hard news. You are on, on, on, making hundreds of decisions, having hundreds of interactions, making hundreds of choices a day that effect your students greatly.

For all of the above reasons, teaching demanded I arrive at my best. The students can sense moods. If I was frustrated about something else, I didn't want my students to think they had done something wrong.

In short, teaching has been hands down, with no comparison, the hardest job I have ever done — with the least pay and prestige.

The buildings are often run-down, the hiring staff at public schools didn't seem at all happy to have hired you, and the district can seem horribly disorganized and unhelpful. In short, you either have to have truly low self-esteem to put up with it, or truly high self-esteem to feel that looking out for the children is worth it.

Often lower pay is offset with a more generous retirement package. But this doesn't initially attract a wider pool of talent to the profession, since few people starting their professions are thinking about retirement.

There are high quality candidates who are able to teach because they are very principled, willing to forego higher pay, or have other sources of money to help compensate.

But the bottom line is this: there would be more candidates to choose from if pay were higher. Teachers who seemed to want to overpower children could languish in the starting gates if the right type of person were screening. Then we won't hear comments such as, "We can't get rid of a PE teacher who swears at elementary students, because you should have seen the previous one, and the ones we have interviewed."

How to help overcome this obstacle?

FIX 1
Support Higher Pay

Parents often spend countless hours raising money to positively amplify their children's school experience. Support using this money for a competitive pay scale to draw teachers to your district.

The more teachers your school has to choose from, the better hires you can make. This flexibility could mean everything to your child.

To put it bluntly, sometimes you get what you pay for. If you want a larger and talented pool of teachers to draw from, they should be well paid.

FIX 2
Propose Your District Accepts Pay Steps from Other Districts

One way to attract a large pool of teachers is to pitch the idea to the PTO and then school board to accept teacher's pay scale or "steps" from previous districts. There are great teachers who want to move with their families for various reasons, and your district will attract them if they don't have to go back to the first step.

FIX 3
Propose Your District Accepts State Transfers

Another way to expand the talent pool: pitch the idea of accepting emergency credentials from state transfers to tap into more talent for the students at your school. There are two emergency credentials. The first is a person who doesn't have a credential yet, but teaches a subject where you need teachers. The second type has a credential in another state. I promise you, it is probably as good as your state's credentials. Again, you will have more candidates, and with proper screening, can get more caring teachers for your children.

FIX 4
Ask Teachers About Their Jobs

Often, when someone asks me what I do, and I say I am a teacher, there is no follow up, or there is some statement that teachers are saints. When you meet teachers in or outside of the classroom, ask them actual questions about their job so they know you are interested. What is hard? What do they like? What do they think about the current curriculum? Testing? To be a great teacher, you need to be more than just a good person, and it is nice to engage with other adults about your profession.

FIX 5
Spearhead a PTO Teacher Appreciation Box or Caring Teacher Award

At a PTO meeting, suggest that your school have a box where parents can complement teachers on acts of caring that could be read at faculty meetings. Or, create a caring educator award and accept nominations from other teachers or students. This sets a caring standard for your school and nudges others towards it. Child kindness is often recognized in this way, and it would be great to have adult kindness as a goal as well. If neither of these fly, ask for other ideas on how you can encourage or recognize teachers who care.

FIX 6
Encourage Successful Teachers to Teach Other Teachers

One year, we had no budget for professional development, so teachers just took turns creating teacher training workshops from conferences they had been to, books they had read, and ideas they had tried that worked. Another no budget approach is to have teachers each share a dilemma in their practice, and discuss it with other teachers. Because these professional development approaches value the expertise already at schools, they can be cost effective and powerful. They also show teachers their expertise is valued.

FIX 7
Get Caring Education Stories Out

Schools should invest in public relations resources to get their successful stories out. Or, members of the PTO with related experience can take this on. Ask teachers to submit to the PR storyteller what they are most excited about in their classroom, that way the fuller picture of what teachers can provide can be told, and meaningful success stories recognized.

These are some practical ways to have more options for caring teachers for your child. Lack of caring can have a different cause — a teacher's core mentality about the reason for teaching.

CAUSE 7
OVERPOWER VS. EMPOWER

When I found myself observing the bully teacher in my master's program, I considered going to ask the advisor if I could be placed with someone different.

Then I thought, if I can just learn what is causing her behavior, I can really learn something here.

So, in our daily debriefs, I began asking this teacher a lot of questions, starting with, "Why did you go into teaching?"

Her answer was a bit rambling, but she described one moment when she realized her students were more scared of her, than she was of them. She said that this was the moment she realized she could stay in teaching.

They are more scared of me than I am of them.

She was talking about first graders. If she is scared of them, she is likely overwhelmed by many situations.

Some adults who feel powerless in their daily lives like having power over small children. In this way, they gain more influence than they might feel at a job working with adults.

Once your classroom door closes, you are the master.

Truly.

Regardless of your skill level, the children, particularly young children, hang on your every word. You have control of almost every minute of their day.

Watching the personalities of bully teachers, I have come to think that some are drawn to teach in order to overpower children.

If I had to I would guess they are continuing some cycle of abuse in their lives, either from home or from their own education. At some point, they were made to feel disempowered. If they are trying to make up for low self-esteem, it is easier to have power over children than adults.

Or the tendency to overpower children can be born of poor teaching skills and classroom management. If you are not prepared, overwhelm students with too many directions, let children run into a classroom before you, do not have a quick way to gain their attention and so forth, you will lose control of the classroom. The classroom will lack a leader, and the students will be silly, talk. Teachers can easily feel disrespected, angry or worse.

The whole school can pretty much see the fiasco walking by your classroom.

One room can be lively, focused and engaged in learning. Another room can be equally lively, but lack focus and clear direction.

A wise teacher re-evaluates their own routines to improve the classroom. They examine their part in the atmosphere they have created. But some don't.

I am in a position to see the same children in our enrichment classes interact with different teachers. Over and over, I have seen two teachers yield very different bounty with the same group of children. With a skilled teacher, they will hang on the teacher's every word, be well behaved, and eager to learn. With another, less skilled teacher, they are wild, disobedient and a bit rude.

If a teacher doesn't rethink the routines to become more successful, s/he may resort to bullying tactics as a last resort to bring order to chaos. It may bring a bit of order, but in a very damaging way to students.

The second type of person attracted to teaching is the polar opposite.

This type of person makes their students want to be more, to do better. They beam at the successes they see and smile at seeing the world through the eyes of a child.

These are the teachers drawn to the profession to empower children.

Colleagues have noted that they see incredibly caring teachers or unkind teachers in school, and surprisingly little in between. Perhaps two opposite personality types are attracted to teaching for exactly opposite reasons.

If overpowering or empowering teachers could be possibly there for your child, how can you find out which type of teacher your child is getting?

FIX 1
Trust Your Intuition

Maya Angelou said, "I've learned that people will forget what you said, people will forget what you did, but people will never forget how you made them feel."

When you walk away from your child's teacher, notice what you feel. Do you feel warm, accepted, welcomed? Or do you feel the teacher is slightly annoyed or impatient with you? Chances are your children feel it a thousand-fold.

Finding caring is a "feel" situation. You feel caring, you don't see or hear it. Someone can say words that sound caring, but they are not truly that caring. They are acting the part. The good news is that people are great at sensing genuine caring, so you really need to trust your intuition here.

FIX 2
Notice Mood around School

Does your child seem happy going to, or being picked up from, school? Few children say they love school, but children with caring teachers are generally fairly happy there. If your child says very negative things about school, or seems kind of miserable there, it is time to play detective.

The most important thing to look for is a decline in your child's self-esteem. If you start hearing things like, "I am terrible at . . ." particularly if it is a subject they previously enjoyed, you need to try to understand what is causing the change.

FIX 3
Do a Face Scan

Walk past your child's classroom before or after drop-off, and look at the children's faces. Do they look happy and engaged? Or quiet and sad? When you walk through the school, keep your ears and eyes open. Often hearing a teacher address a child in a hall is enough to give you a clue.

FIX 4
Inquire About Philosophy

At back to school night or a conference, here are some questions you can ask that can give insight into the teacher's relationships with students:

- Why did you decide to become a teacher?
- How do you think your experience as a student impacts how you teach?
- What is your philosophy on classroom management?

FIX 5
Notice How the Teacher Talks About Your Child

In one-on-one conversations, if the teacher cares about your child, the teacher is going to naturally begin conversations with very specific strengths that they see in your child, or share stories and anecdotes. If the teacher cares about your child, the stories they share may not always be totally flattering, but they are shared in a spirit of amusement. If this part seems forced and fake, like something they know they should do in order to segue into criticism, then they probably are being forced and fake. If the strengths are simply skipped at all points of contact, your child is likely not in a very caring environment. Teachers who share frustration about children who are just being children — energetic, daydreamy — may not be as caring.

FIX 6
Volunteer to Observe and Gain Empathy

Try to volunteer. Watch what teachers say in the whole group and one-on-one to the class. Remember, children take teacher's remarks to heart, particularly in the younger grades. How would you feel hearing the comments if you were young?

FIX 7
Check Out Work Feedback

Look for assignments where you can't tell what the teacher really wants, and the child seems stressed. This can be a sign of an overly controlling and critical teacher.

Notice feedback on child's work. How would you feel reading it? Would you feel encouraged or discouraged?

If the child wants to the please the teacher, but has no fear or stress associated with it, this is a great sign of positive attachment to the teacher.

FIX 8
Alert the Principal

If you see a frustrated teacher, who has poor classroom management, you may want to suggest the principal provide feedback or training. You may want to do this discretely to help the teacher be more successful, without drawing repercussions.

CAUSE 8
"TO TEACH WELL IS TO FIND FLAWS" MENTALITY

Some teachers believe that their job is to point out deficits only. To find these deficits, they don't compare children to a typical child of that age, but they compare the child to a perfect adult. These are the deflators. To help your child with a deflator, try the following.

FIX 1
Set the Stage for Caring

When you first meet with your child's new teacher, or the teacher asks you to send a note about your child, say or write something like this: *My child needs a kind, caring atmosphere to learn. I want my child to understand his or her strengths, as well as have realistic goals to work on.*

Before you have any interactions, you have announced clear expectations for what your child needs to learn and be happy in school.

FIX 2
Give Your Child Perspective on the Little Things

If your child shares that a teacher is picking on small things, ask yourself, in the big scheme of life, is this as important or stressful as my child's teacher is making it? If not, help your child put it in perspective.

Say, "Yes, it is not great to wrinkle work too much, as it can be hard to read, but it happens sometimes. It is not the end of the world."

If the teacher sends back kindergarten papers bleeding with red for spelling, and they are trying to learn to spell, you can give them another way to look at it.

You can have them listen to a baby learn to talk. Ask your child,

"Do you stop the baby and correct them each time they say "tuck" instead of truck? No, you smile and encourage them to talk more, and model saying truck correctly. That is the way to teach a child to speak."

Ask your child if it makes sense that a kindergartner would know how to spell every word when they are learning to spell. Tell them that you are proud if they know that "m" makes the "em" sound, and that this is an important part of learning to spell.

If your young child gets in trouble for talking, let them know that it is wise not to talk when the teacher is talking, but it is also normal for this to be difficult to do, because it is hard not to say what you are thinking.

Whatever the issue is, replace a critical, non-caring voice with a supportive, caring one. Take the time and energy to create a healthy inner dialogue for your child.

You are keeping the goals as goals, explaining why they might be emphasized, but also framing the relative importance it should have in your child's overall self-esteem.

FIX 3
Set Goals for Positive Feedback

A teacher deflator is likely to set up a conference with you at some point to complain, and it is best if you request the conference first. Otherwise, your needs can seem defensive, and the conversation may not go as well.

Set up the conference, ideally outside of conference week. During conference week, teachers are literally drinking out of a firehose. They are trying to prepare report cards, portfolios, make the class look really nice, have several intense fast paced meetings a day, and teach, often all in the same day. Also, if you set it up at a different time, the teacher will be more focused, and understand that you are concerned.

Start by helping them see the cup as at least half full. Say something like, "I am wondering what you see as my child's strengths." This flips the script and sets an expectation of noticing strengths, which might nudge the teacher to see your child in a new light. Then ask the teacher if they can share these strengths with your child more, as it will help them know what they are good at.

If the teacher cannot point out strengths, ask the teacher if they can help your child be happier in school, by getting to know them better, and helping them identify strengths.

If your child's perspective is that the teacher doesn't like them, and that the teacher is mainly just frustrated with them, share that. (With older children, get permission from them first.) Hearing that gives most teachers pause, and makes them want to change tack. Explain that you are worried that your child is being overwhelmed with criticisms that could lead your child to shut down in the classroom.

If the teacher keeps going on about faults that are small and common to many children, help frame it for the teacher: "My child is by nature forgetful, active, day dreamy and so forth." But point to the flip side of these traits. Forgetful children are often very in the moment, active energy is healthy. Give specific suggestions on how feedback can be framed in a less harsh way, or put into better perspective, that will set your child up for success.

If a teacher complains that a child is not doing exactly what the teacher wants, ask exactly what the teacher wants, or ask if you can come see what s/he is talking about.

If the teacher is not able to be very reflective in the moment, just ask if it is something s/he can be more attentive to, since every child is different. Keep connecting with your child, and deciding if it is worth following up on. Teachers with any love of children will have been sad to upset a child, and will carefully consider and revise.

Keep following up with this clear goal in mind for your child: My child needs a kind, caring atmosphere to learn. I want my child to understand his or her strengths, as well as have realistic goals to work on. Are you hearing and seeing improvement, or not? Let them know either way. Be persistent!

Sometimes, generally caring teachers do randomly uncaring things. Typically, there is a hot spot from their childhood — something they were shamed for that didn't match the rest of the way they were treated. If a generally caring teachers does this, you are in good shape if you have been thanking them. Simply point out how confused and sad it made your child feel. They are likely to reflect and improve if it is out of character for them.

CAUSE 9
PROTECTION FOR TEACHER-BULLIES

Over the years, teacher friends have shared with me things they have heard other bully teachers say to students, all at schools that are considered strong schools in the community.

- If only your parents cared about your education.
- You are stupid like your mother.
- I can do whatever I want to you, and there is nothing you can do about it.
- You are a "disgusting little worm."

So why are these teachers still teaching?

I started learning why during my hiring interview for a public school.

The human resources person said, "You will be probationary at first."

"What is probationary?" I asked.

"It is what you are before you are tenured," came the reply.

"Tenured?" I asked.

I had associated the word "tenured" with university professors doing research that needed to be protected. How did tenure relate to my teaching elementary school?

"How do you get tenure?" I asked.

"Basically, just get to school on time, and don't leave before you are supposed to, and you will be tenured," came the reply, sprinkled with a hint of sarcasm.

"Okay," I said, insulted by these pathetically low expectations, and still not really understanding what he was saying.

What I eventually came to understand was that because of tenure, and myriad union protections for teachers, tenured teachers really can't be fired.

If districts try to remove teachers, the laws are stacked against them. The legal fees can run between $50,000 and $450,000 for one case — money the district typically doesn't have — and the teacher is still not fired.

Your child then has a higher risk of encountering a bullying teacher; they are not weeded out of the profession.

This is a huge deal for principals tasked with creating quality schools.

As a new teacher, what I heard repeated from older teachers, was different forms of: "What are they going to do — fire me?" How does one manage — given that truth?

Generally, the most the principal can do is move the teacher around to different grades, in an effort to annoy the teacher and hope that s/he leaves.

Doctors vow to "do no harm." And if they do, a complaint can be filed, the governing board investigates, and they can lose their license.

For teachers it is different.

There is a governing board for licenses (teacher credentialing commissions), but somehow it has evolved that they do not seem to have real power to take complaints, investigate, require steps to keep your license, or possibly revoke a license.

What about private schools, where there is no tenure for teachers? Sadly, sometimes they choose to look the other way when children are being treated poorly.

Why would they do this?

First, it is often hard to believe teachers are bullying, because they can be good at presenting a more pleasant face with adults.

Second, the private school may have slowly normalized this behavior as acceptable. Many parents choose private schools to have stronger discipline, and many bully teachers describe themselves as strong disciplinarians. This reinforces a culture that the school actually prides itself on.

Third, if the private teacher is fired and people start talking about why, the school is getting "bad press." So, the school may try to downplay or avoid the situation.

A parent shared with me the story of a private school unwilling to investigate her elementary school daughter's account of being forced to dress up in tights, while a male teacher photographed her. In the face of administrative inaction by the principal (a legally mandated reporter), the mother threatened to call the police herself. With that threat, the school contacted the authorities, but downplayed the incident to the broader school community and press, most probably to maintain the school's reputation. The police investigation revealed thousands of sexually explicit photos and videos of young student victims on the teacher's electronic devices, which led to multiple felony convictions and a six-year sentence in state prison.

Given these institutional protections for teachers who shouldn't be around children, how do you protect your child from being hurt?

You might feel: What in the world can I do about union or teaching credentialing issues?

My response is this: The love of a parent for a child is a powerful force. Parents spend countless hours on school events, but if they used their efforts more strategically, much more would improve for their children. Parents may get involved, but not in a direction that truly makes a difference in their child's education. Parents are an unharnessed force for improvement. Once you understand the barriers, there are clever ways to persistently try to overcome them strategically and educate others to do the same.

FIX 1
Ask to Have a Parent on the School's
Interviewing Committee

Your first goal is to try to prevent your child from being placed with a teacher who shouldn't be teaching, because they hurt, rather than help, children. Here's how:

Ask to have at least one parent on the interviewing committee at your school. Make sure a hands-on lesson is part of the interview process. Notice how the teacher connects with children. Are they kind? Do they seem irritated at all by children? Ask that kindness be a large determining factor in the hiring process.

FIX 2
Request Teachers If Needed

As soon as possible in the school year, start asking parents and students what the teachers are like for the following year. Just as with your child, when speaking with other parents or students, use "tell me more" and ask for examples to determine if a teacher is caring.

If you like your child's current teacher, ask them which teacher would be the best fit for your child next year. Kind teachers usually recommend other kind teachers.

If all of the teachers in the upcoming grade seem caring, then your work is done, and you don't need to make a request.

If only a few seem caring, or you hear that one is really unkind, advocate for a kind teacher for your child. Here are the best steps to make the request. This may seem a bit detailed, but when you understand how the process works, the details matter.

- Make your request by February the year before, as the work creating class lists can start as early as March.

- Make your first request in person with the principal. The basic communication is this: "My child needs to feel safe to learn, and I want these teachers, or not these teachers, as a result." Tell your principal that you think your child will thrive with these teachers, and be unhappy and learn less with others. If there are stories and examples making you request not to have a teacher, the principal should know them. The principal, at both private and public schools will likely respond that the class has to be created to balance sexes, academic ability etc. and that they cannot honor your request. All of this is true, but in reality, they do often try to honor the request. You are trying to prevent a problem before it starts.

- After that meeting, you should follow this up with a written request with the standard, "X teachers would be the best fit for my child, given his or her learning needs." The written request should contain no more than that, as teachers often read these requests while making class lists. If you write every detail about why you don't want a teacher, and the teacher reads it, and your child ends up with that teacher anyway, you are not in a good situation.

Some in education might say, "I can't believe you would suggest that parents request teachers. This will make it so difficult for schools, who already have so many challenges."

I don't suggest that all parents request teachers. I advise this only if you have reason to believe that your child will be placed with a teacher who will hurt your child. If schools were allowed to have the same employment rules as the rest of the country, these teachers would have been already asked to leave, and you wouldn't have to worry. You could rest assured that all the adults that interacted with your child had their best interests at heart, even if they weren't perfect. But we are not yet in that world, and the negative impact on your child is too great not to advocate on their behalf.

The truth is that many teachers request teachers for their own children. They know how important a caring teacher is for their child's development.

Your goal is not to be difficult. Your goal is to help your child get a good education by trying to get the most caring teacher you can for your child. Even if the other pieces of a great education aren't solidly in place, your child will at least be happy under a caring teacher. Much more learning follows from that.

If you are creating discomfort in the school by requesting a caring teacher, it should give the school pause about why so many parents want that certain teacher, and don't want others. Hopefully, raising the expectations will inch things in the right direction.

But what can you do if you are past the point you can request, and you start to feel your child is in the teacher bullying arena?

Listen for things that would shame, embarrass, or make a child feel something is wrong with them. These are difficult feelings to shake, and need the most attention.

If you aren't sure if it is bullying, ask yourself, if another child was in a position of power, and doing this to my child, would I think it is bullying?

The other important thing to look at is your child's happiness and confidence. If you have noticed a huge change, something is causing it. If your child seems happy, but reports comments that you aren't sure about, perhaps the teacher has a dry sense of humor and the class gets it. So, take into account what your child reports, and also how your child seems.

If you don't see an issue, I would suggest you skip the rest of this chapter. It is a lot of detail to read if you aren't in the situation, and you can always come back to it if the situation arises, but I hope it does not.

FIX 3
Remain as Calm as You Can

If there is an issue, it is going to be hard and upsetting, but here is how you can best help your child given the constraints in place.

If you hear something upsetting, you will feel very angry. But try to remain calm enough so that you can still think, and not overwhelm your child. Be genuine in your reaction, but soothe yourself enough to soothe your child. *This is not okay, but we will figure everything out and it will be okay.* That is the basic message.

FIX 4
Gather Information

If you start hearing things that you feel are not right, try to find out more from those around you to get the bigger picture.

Ask both students and parents what the teacher is like. If you hear or notice something strange, ask more questions. Sometimes it is the answer to the sixth question from another child, rather than your child, that tells you what you need to know.

Our son once had a strange interaction with a gym teacher who said that if our son caught a certain number of passes in the football game, he would take him out to dinner. The teacher wasn't the coach of the team. He was just watching the game. He would comment on exactly how many yards our son would run, and our son was not the star of the team. This was something our son mentioned in passing.

One day, our son mentioned that this gym teacher repeated a trick the students played on each other, but he did it to our son. The students would step and hold down one foot and push the person backwards, not in anger, but as a joke. The teacher did this to our son in front of the whole class, as if he were a fellow student.

I asked our son's friend in the back seat, while driving them around, what he thought about this teacher. The friend had been at the school longer. He kept saying that he is weird, strange, off, but nothing specific.

I kept asking, "What specifically does he do that makes you think he is weird?"

Finally, when we had parked, and my son and his friend were leaving to get out of the car, my son's friend said, "One time my friend was working out in the gym at school and the teacher grabbed right by his you know (motioning to his crotch), and said, 'that exercise works out these muscles.'"

Okay, that is something a child might not be comfortable sharing at first, and certainly important to know. This coupled with what the teacher was saying and doing, needed to be acted upon. Had I not calmly and repeatedly kept asking, I would never have known.

You should always be respectful, thoughtful, and dig deep to find out what is really going on, and not jump to conclusions. Your questions should be open ended, not leading, to clarify what you do not understand.

Teachers that are generally kind are almost universally praised as such by students. Children are staunch defenders of kind teachers.

There is always the fear that a child could say something un-true about a teacher, maybe in retaliation for something, or to get attention. So as with anything, this can swing too far in the oppo-site direction.

Let's go back to the child bullying analogy. You don't want to go back to accepting basic torture from peers as normal. But it is too far in the other direction when children say they have been bullied because someone tells them to shut up once.

So, check to be sure you are getting a clear story. If bullying is occurring, typically, multiple students are witnessing it. Double check. This is someone's life and reputation, so you want to be sure of your information. The bullying is occurring in a full classroom, not in a dark side alley.

And remember "strict" and "bully" are different things. Having clear but realistic expectations and enforcing them fairly is strict. It raises children up. Bullying, on the other hand, flattens children.

FIX 5
Name It

If what your child shares is abusive or wrong, whether or not it happened to your child or another child, name it as so. Make it clear it is unacceptable, and that no child deserves this treatment.

FIX 6
Plan with Your Child

I have encountered students who should be telling their parents and teachers about something going on at school that is really serious. But they do not tell their parents.

When we discover it another way, and ask why they didn't say something, the answer often goes something like this, "My parents will just freak out and make a big deal over it."

I am not certain, but I think this is a child's way of saying that they have completely lost control of past situations like this, and don't want it to happen again.

If you complained to your spouse about something at work and found out the next day that your spouse had called your work without telling you, and complained about the situation, how would you feel? It really isn't so different. So, start planning with your child, if possible.

With younger children, say K - 2nd graders, you can likely take on the planning unilaterally.

From 3rd grade on, as upset as you probably are, and as much as you just want to rush into the school, you want to handle this in a way that feels okay to your child.

Your first instinct, most likely, if the bullying is extreme, will be to ask for the teacher's removal, explaining exactly the damage the teacher has caused.

In private schools, and with non-tenured public school teachers, you may get somewhere with this request. With a public school tenured teacher, you will not get them removed due to laws and unions protecting them.

So, what to do? For an answer, look to the problem of child bullies.

Child bullies, like teacher bullies, often can't be removed from schools. However, outing them and letting them know adults and students are watching and talking are the two most powerful strategies to make the behavior stop. So that is your goal with the teacher.

Usually when a more mundane problem arises, I advocate going to the teacher first to establish a healthy dialogue.

However, with a teacher bully, if you go to the teacher first, the teacher will likely try to talk to the principal before you do, with a counter story. They may even scare your child into changing the story before it gets to the principal.

You are also going to need protection, so that your child does not get backlash for telling. The principal should be able to protect your child.

So, if you suspect teacher bullying, I suggest meeting with the principal first.

Here are some options:

- **Simply Report to the Principal.** Say to your child, "Your teacher is being a teacher-bully, and it is wrong, and needs to stop, for the sake of all the children in the class." Tell them bullies often think people won't tell, but once people do, they realize they have to stop. Say that you know the principal does not like things like this. Propose simply telling first, so the child doesn't feel there is anything wrong with calling out bad behavior. If the child is fine with it, then go with it. If the child reacts poorly, draw them out. What are they afraid of? It could be quite valid. If they don't like this first suggestion, try the next one.

- **Go to the Principal but Don't Share the Source of the Information.** If your child doesn't like the idea of telling the principal, ask how s/he would feel if you shared that you just overheard children talking about things the teacher does, but that you won't share who you heard it from. It could be from any student in the class, since they all saw it. This might be the best strategy because the goal is to out the behavior. The teacher will not try to silence more than one child. If you imply it was at a game, or birthday party, without exactly saying that, it could have been any child talking about it, not just your child's friends, that is even better. Most children will accept this second solution as one that keeps them safe.

- **Go to the Principal Anonymously.** If your child is still uncomfortable with that idea, you can propose this: "I will ask that the principal not tell the teacher that I was the parent that shared the information. So, the teacher will not connect it to you. I will tell the principal I overheard it, and the principal will not like it and will tell the teacher to stop. This way, the information should not be linked with the child at all.

- **Send an Anonymous Letter.** The final proposal to your child, if they are worried about the information being linked to them, might be to have you send an anonymous letter to the principal, saying you have heard that x teacher is using bullying tactics on students, such as screaming, ripping papers, saying very cutting things, and that it needs to stop. You can phrase it in a generic enough way, so it is not linked to your child. Explain that you are communicating it this way, as your child is scared of the teacher.

For all these proposals, if your child's reaction is against any telling at first, give them a few days, and re-explain the option that might be the closest to their comfort level. Sometimes, like adults, they need time to reflect and balance bravery with strategy.

Explain what a good thing you are doing, so that no other children have to go through this. But that you want to be smart and do it in a way that they feel comfortable with.

Also, share your story with other parents, if you can keep your child's confidentiality, if your child has requested that. Just say you heard this was happening, but don't say to whom, if necessary. Ask around. If others have had similar experiences, see if they will join you in the meeting. Sometimes principals say this is the first they are hearing of a behavior, when that is really not the case. If previous complaining parents are in the meeting, there is strength in numbers.

If your child asks you not to say anything in any way shape or form, particularly an older child, try to continue the conversation with him or her, but respect their wishes. Your child is the one having to face the teacher day in and day out.

Older children are much better than younger children at seeing teachers' behavior as a failing of the teacher, rather than the student. They will have picked up emotional strategies to protect themselves. In addition, unlike elementary school, they generally switch to many different teachers, so no one teacher will hold the same sway that an elementary teacher does. Regardless, an older child still needs to hear loudly and clearly from you the same refrain any child needs to hear about abusive behavior: It is not your fault (or your friend's fault) and no one deserves to be treated this way.

But continue to problem solve. This is wrong. How can we make it better? Listen to their ideas too. Sometimes children are more motivated to protect other children than themselves. Explain that the teacher will keep doing this to students if you don't try to stop it.

This strategizing provides useful life skills for any future times your child may need to confront someone in a position of authority in a way that minimizes backlash.

Once you have your plan, you can move forward.

FIX 7
Meet with the Principal

If the plan involves meeting with the school, here are a few tips on that next step:

If you are in a private school, and your child is witnessing a bully teacher, or being bullied by a teacher, you have every reason to expect that the teacher is not in the profession. But if you are in a public school and the teacher has tenure, the principal really can't fire them.

The difficulty this can present for a principal is huge. And principals know it, and so are stuck when receiving complaints. You might as well acknowledge that you know this up front, and not beat your head against a wall. So, don't be mad at the principal. It really is not their fault, and they probably feel as frustrated as you do.

Remember, your goal is to out the teacher and let them know you are watching.

Write down notes, of exactly what you agreed to with your child, so you won't be carried away with emotion and forget. If your child wants the principal to not share which parent complained, then start the meeting by saying you want the conversation off the record, and don't want the complaint linked back to you. Explain that your child is afraid of teacher backlash. If they can't agree, then end the meeting.

And then, again, using the details of the plan, explain that you want this to stop, and call it bullying if it is. Explain that your child fears the teacher, and you want to protect your child from backlash.

If a child were using a position of power to embarrass other children, what would the school do? Would you allow a student to yell at another student or rip up their work? Then why should a principal accept this behavior from a teacher?

FIX 8
Meet with the Teacher

If you have not set up the meeting as anonymous, the principal will likely suggest a meeting with the teacher. I would insist that the principal be present.

Discuss the possibility of backlash: "I am going to talk to you about this, and I will be watching for any unkind treatment of my child as a result."

Tell the teacher what you have learned. If it is not about your child, tell them you don't want your child witnessing this type of bullying behavior. Explain what you heard, and what the impact is.

Tell them you want it to stop. If it is not kind or caring, it should not be done. It hurts children.

Depending on your trust level with the teacher, you may ask the teacher to apologize to the child, or if your child is very shy, not to bring it up with the child.

FIX 9
Volunteer Frequently

The message? I am watching. Ask other parents to report to you how your child is being treated.

FIX 10
Follow Up

Now here comes the most important part. If you have done an intervention with the school to protect your child, and you have included your child in a way they feel safe, then you are in a good position. Your child should feel safe enough to follow up with you. Be positive. You want your child to feel they live in a good world, so say, "Your teacher said she feels bad she was unkind, and is going to try to be nicer, so notice what s/he does that is nice or not nice."

- What was a nice thing your teacher did today?
- Was there anything not nice that your teacher did today or that you aren't sure about?

Depending on the initial plan, follow up. You may feel exhausted, and just wish this will get better. But it is a marathon, not a sprint.

It may take 2-3 times for the teacher to really feel their behavior is noticed. Consider other options you may not have considered at first, including moving your child's class, or if you really have lost faith in the school's response — a new school. Your child may resist such a transition, due to familiarity and friends. Making new friends can be a child's least favorite thing to do. Respect that, but continue to let them know it is an option to think about.

If you are not having any luck bringing change this way, you may want to consider the following options.

FIX 11
Alert the Credentialing Commission

The teacher credentialing department should monitor teachers that need more oversight, or shouldn't hold a teaching license. Try to submit complaints there, and if the process is unwieldy, find out who is in charge of the commission in your state (often the governor). Complain to who is in charge. Research the commission. How many complaints are filed? Does the commission take action?

FIX 12
Educate Other Parents

Many parents don't know how teacher tenure or teacher credentialing commissions work. Since you know this, make sure other parents, neighbors, parent-teacher organization and community do as well.

FIX 13
Research Before Voting

When voting, really read. Union PR and lobbying often message legislation as "anti-teacher." Read further. Is it really anti-teacher, or is it pro-child? Discuss this with other parents, so they have all the facts about the impact of legislation on their child.

FIX 14
Write Reviews and Ratings

Go to sites that accept reviews on schools or teachers, and write specifically and directly what you have heard or observed about any teachers at the school. Don't be a bystander that turns a blind eye. Some pressure is better than no pressure at all.

FIX 15
Notify Child Protective Services

I got this idea from a principal. She got a report regarding abusive teacher behavior. Knowing her limitations, the principal called in a report to the child protective services. It led to an investigation, which surely sent the teacher a message. Again, the goal is to have the behavior outed.

FIX 16
Don't Cover Up

If private schools feel you will cover for and protect the teacher, they may not act. Make sure they know that the behavior will be outed to the community to encourage action.

Hopefully, these items will move you closer to caring teachers for your child's education.

Now let's look at the second "C" — **Connected Curriculum**.

What is your child learning in school?

PART II

THE SECOND "C"

–CONNECTED CURRICULUM–

WHAT I HAVE SEEN

At a second student teaching placement, I visited a class doing a Writer's Workshop and walked into a room full of passion. The first graders were beyond excited. One begged to sit with me and read me her chapter book on slavery. I was blown away. At the end of class, the students confidently sat in the author's chair, read their stories to the class, and called on peers to get feedback.

This is going to be the kind of classroom I create someday, I thought.

And yet, my first classroom couldn't have been further from this.

My first job was as a third-grade long-term substitute teacher. The teacher told me the exact page number of each text and workbook that the students were to be on when she returned. The texts and worksheets were all drill and kill. You barely had to think to complete them.

I felt like a robot reading the workbook page instructions. I tried to have the class do the pages extra quickly to carve out time for interesting projects. But the pages did take time, and I had promised her the students would be on a certain page when she returned.

It felt alien, reading the dry instructions. Though I loved the students, I was clearly boring them. The faces looking at me were sad and tired. They looked miserable, and they were learning very little. I knew it. They knew it.

I had gone into education to prevent children from having the boring experience my brother and I had in elementary school, so this made it all the worse.

I would like to say I never saw those same bored faces again after this teaching experience, and I did not — not in my own classrooms.

But walking around schools, I saw these bored faces over and over again.

At private schools, public schools, highly rated schools, and poorly rated schools, high income schools and low-income schools, over and over.

Working through my Master of Teaching program, I had learned about closed ended, low level regurgitation worksheets, like they were a thing of the past. They weren't.

Here is the basic drill, which I probably don't need to tell you, as you probably have experienced it:

The students are assigned to read a certain number of pages from a dry textbook and answer recall questions at the end of the section. Photosynthesis is . . . What is photosynthesis? Many times, it is basically copying the paragraph from the text. Then students do related workbook pages, which involve the same basic copying or recall.

There is a place for some of this low-level recall, when you need to memorize math facts for example, after you have learned the concept of multiplication.

The problem is that some teachers apply this low-level recall to all of their lessons, and to all of their subjects.

I remember helping a first grader tediously copy sentences from his text for a workbook page, only to flip to the next assignment asking for the very same sentences. He looked like he was going to cry.

I have seen students copying long definitions in tiny print, or copying twenty words ten times each, that they already knew how to spell.

I have seen children who can read chapter books completing worksheets asking them to draw lines between the letter B and ball.

Now, textbooks don't necessarily have to be dry, and the worksheets don't necessarily have to be recall; they could ask much more robust questions. But the reality is that the texts typically *are* dry and the questions *do* focus on regurgitation.

Many classrooms are still overly focused on the bottom two rungs of this chart outlining levels of thinking:

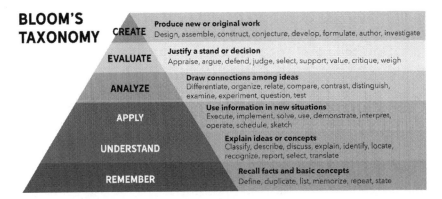

BLOOM'S TAXONOMY

CREATE — Produce new or original work
Design, assemble, construct, conjecture, develop, formulate, author, investigate

EVALUATE — Justify a stand or decision
Appraise, argue, defend, judge, select, support, value, critique, weigh

ANALYZE — Draw connections among ideas
Differentiate, organize, relate, compare, contrast, distinguish, examine, experiment, question, test

APPLY — Use information in new situations
Execute, implement, solve, use, demonstrate, interpret, operate, schedule, sketch

UNDERSTAND — Explain ideas or concepts
Classify, describe, discuss, explain, identify, locate, recognize, report, select, translate

REMEMBER — Recall facts and basic concepts
Define, duplicate, list, memorize, repeat, state

The education battlefield has two camps related to Bloom's Taxonomy. They go by different names at different times, but the war is the same.

It pits content oriented, traditional education vs. process oriented, progressive education.

The content oriented, traditional camp favors memorizing basic facts and knowing basic skills before doing more creative work.

The process oriented, progressive camp feels that this content is not as important. They feel your child should be applying, analyzing, evaluating, and creating all along, using the content that is most interesting to them.

Here is what the traditional side says about progressive side: You can't just study whatever you want. There needs to be core knowledge that we all possess. What are they even learning?

Here is what the progressive side says about traditional side: We live in a different age. Memorizing and regurgitating a bunch of information is not useful. Computers can replace that kind of knowledge. We need thinkers, creators, innovators; and they need to learn by doing.

Traditionalists favor phonics in reading first (practicing the letter sounds).

Progressives favor whole language (reading actual books).

Traditionalists favor memorizing standard algorithms for math. Progressives favor understanding math concepts as the more important goal.

Most schools **say** they teach both process and content skills.

If you want to see your school's process skills, they are generally outlined in the school's mission statement.

The school's content skills are listed in the school standards, which will be either national standards or state standards.

But in reality, many schools skew towards just teaching the content. They spend much less time on experiences that build process skills.

There are some progressive, usually private, schools that go quite far in the other direction, all process, with very little set content to cover. They let children learn whatever they are interested in. If they want to study caterpillars for a semester, they let them.

I partially agree with both sides, and take a centrist approach.

There are facts and basic information that should be common knowledge. If a child graduates school, and has no idea that heat rises, then they don't have basic common sense about where to place a heater to warm their room, or won't understand how weather and ocean currents work. Meeting someone and realizing what was happening in history when that person was growing up creates points of understanding. Being able to quickly figure out a tip at a restaurant is useful. I could go on. So yes, certain content and skills are important.

But we all know that if you are just book smart, but lack other skills such as creativity, real-life problem-solving skills, perseverance, or excellent communication, you won't get very far.

Furthermore, just because you know something doesn't mean you can do it.

For example, you can know that calming yourself to better handle a stressful situation is important to be a good leader. I can tell you that, and one second later you could answer a multiple-choice question about it correctly on a test.

But being able to actually do it when the stressful situation strikes? Well, that is a different story. And that requires lots of practice and reflection in actual stressful scenarios. This reality favors teaching process skills.

The win-win is that when you teach content skills using important process skills, you get the benefit of learning both. Think back to what you have memorized for tests over the years and what you have retained of that information. The creative part of learning is what makes the learning stick.

Let's look more closely at children using disconnected vs. connected curriculum, and what the results might be.

WHY IT MATTERS

"My goodness they are spoiled," I thought.

When I was a first year teacher, I was spending hours giving my students what I wished I had had as a student – hands on science. The only problem was — the students. They wouldn't listen to my directions. They complained about it, saying things like, "Are we done yet?"

I grumbled to myself as I cleaned up all the materials and missed my lunch break.

I ruminated more: These kids don't appreciate how good they have it, and how much work I am doing for them.

And that was almost the end of it.

But I managed to remember that these same "spoiled" students were tremendously grateful for our Writer's Workshop curriculum. They begged me to do it, and showed great appreciation for the time.

They didn't act "spoiled" then.

So why did they act "spoiled" during my science curriculum and not my writing curriculum?

In that moment, I switched from a blaming stance to a curious stance. And that is when I started to figure out why these lessons were so bumpy.

During the Writer's Workshop they loved, the students could create, edit, and publish their books. There was structure in the process, but they had a lot of control in creating and refining the project.

But when I thought about my science class, though it was hands-on, it was really just a more elaborate way to follow very specific and controlled directions:

"Put a drop, wait, stop, hands on your head."

They were marched in sync to all get to the same prescribed "discovery."

I decided to try to apply what I thought made Writer's Workshop work to my science class. The class needed a challenge that really asks the child to bring problem solving to the table, a level of autonomy to create, and sharing time to learn as a community. I decided to call it Experimenter's Workshop. Writers write. Scientists experiment.

I would encourage the students to design their own experiments to answer questions. Instead of featured authors, the children would be featured scientists sharing what they did, noticed, and theories.

We were studying states of matter, so I asked the question: "What melts ice the fastest: baking soda, salt, or water?" Basic supplies were provided, and the children were to design an experiment to find out. They had to write their results for Featured Scientists.

The class was like night and day with this new approach. They almost immediately grasped the importance of controlling independent variables, such as the size of the ice cubes, the timing of applying the "melting" ingredients and so forth. They loved it and begged for Experimenter's Workshop. They said "thanks." A lot.

Their behavior and the amount they were learning both changed dramatically for the better.

Experimenter's Workshop was born, along with the idea of applying these basic principles in other areas: reading, math, art, and study skills during Workshop Education enrichment classes.

That moment, I think, was the most important one of my entire time in education.

Because I moved past my original "spoiled" theory, and moved into designing learning that matched children's traits, I had very different children on my hands.

Misbehavior is often a sign that learning experiences have been poorly designed.

Let's say your child has an overabundance of low-level recall work. Here are some of the things you can expect:

Almost all children dislike mindless repetitive recall work when they are given too much of it. Active children, bright children, imaginative children, and headstrong children really have a negative reaction to it.

I sense that children often become angry when a day unfolds like this, but they don't know why they are angry. Children often express anger about this by misbehaving. Or they try to entertain themselves when they are bored.

They don't think, "This type of curriculum is boring me."

They think, "I hate school and learning." Unless they are given more perspective, they think their experience is what school and learning is. Period.

In addition, behaviors that would not even be noticed in a high-level thinking class can be cause for getting in trouble in a low-level thinking class.

For example, a kinetic, talkative child, who moves a lot, will not stand out in a class with higher level thinking and hands-on project learning.

This same kinetic, talkative child could get in a ton of trouble if the expectation is silently filling out worksheets most of the day.

If your child is working silently, in isolation, which is generally how children do low level work, they will feel more socially anxious at school.

So, what is better? Connected Curriculum.

Here are important qualities of connected curriculum.

- **Higher Level Thinking Skills**: Basic recall and understanding assignments are generally less interesting to do than those that involve applying knowledge or using knowledge to create something new.

- **Choice**: The more choice you give most people, the more invested they are in their work and decisions, and children are no different. Designing an experiment to learn which syrup is thicker is a richer learning experience than just following experiment directions that someone has already written.

- **Sense of Purpose**: Checking writing for capital letters and periods to publish a book (the larger purpose) will be more motivating than finding grammar mistakes in random sentences on a worksheet.

- **Feedback:** If there is the assurance that a peer or an adult, will really notice the work and give a strength and maybe a question or suggestion, you will have a much more motivated worker. Aren't we all this way?

- **Social Skills:** This means lessons have a balance of team, partner or solo work. If your child is, at least part of the time, working with partners or in groups on interesting projects, they will feel a part of a connected community. I have seen children become connected in friendship when they try to build a difficult bridge together, or team up to write a book together. These meaningful learning goals bond them, and give them social security.

- **Goals:** There should be very clear goals about the purpose of the time. Whether it is writing the best story introduction possible, or creating a new line up procedure to come in from recess faster, students should know the goal, how success will be measured, and that they will keep working until they meet it.

Here are some examples of substitutions for low level recall worksheet learning:

K-3

- **Learning letter-sound connections:** Children work solo or as a team to make an alphabet book. You can have the option of having a theme: dinosaurs, dance moves, etc. Students share work-in-progress with the class, and get feedback as they work.

- **Counting to 100, or skipping counting:** Collect a hundred acorns for the squirrels and make a squirrel food stand. Collect 100 leaves that birds can use in their nests, and a make a bird nest stand. Collect 100 branches and see what you can build out of it. For younger children, just gaining fluency in counting to 100 will be the first step. If counting to 100 is easy, then start learning to count by 2's, 5's, 10's and so forth. After the children collect items, ask how they can prove to you that they have collected 100. This should encourage them to group them in groups of 2's,

5's or 10's. If they don't think of this, suggest it, and triple check the counting by counting by 2's, 5's, or 10's, if they are ready for this concept.

K-8

- **Reading comprehension:** Book club. Read out loud to younger students, or have older students read the same book. Discuss one or more of the following questions below. These are all strategies that excellent readers use, from *Mosaic of Thought* by Keene and Zimmerman.

    - **What do you wonder just from the cover?** This activates questions and encourages a more careful reading of the text to find answers or prove or disprove theories.

    - **What questions do you have about the book?** Good readers notice when they are confused and use clues and further thought to try to figure it out.

    - **Does anything in the book remind you of anything in your own life?** Connecting the text to your own experiences provides a deeper reading experience.

    - **Does anything in the book remind you of anything in another book or movie?** As children get older, this can expand more abstract concepts like theme for discussion.

    - **Summarizing.** If you had to explain the main point of this book in three sentences, what would you say?

- **Writing:** Make a book. Take a few pages of white paper and staple them or bend them in half. It doesn't need to look fancy. At its most basic, the teacher and class brainstorm book ideas, the child writes a simple book, reads it to the class as a featured author, and calls on students to share strengths and questions/suggestions. As students get more advanced, teachers can add editing checklists that must be completed before the child shares as featured author. Books can be displayed in class as silent reading options.

- **Addition, subtraction, multiplication, division, or any math skills like fractions:** First have children master facts and computation, by encouraging them to create memory devices to help them with those facts that are hard for them to remember quickly. Once the basics are mastered, the student can work solo or in a team to make a math board game for the class to play that also teaches the math skill. This example makes use of a "drill and kill" worksheet, but instead of doing them over and over, you have a clear goal – to teach yourself memory tricks as needed, and then once they are mastered, to increase fluency with your invented board game.

- **Integrated Learning — Math and Writing and. . .** Have students start a company, and sell their goods or experiences to each other or the wider community. Students can promote, set pricing, and do test runs to get feedback. Students can use profits to shop at each other's companies.

All of these examples require higher level thinking skills and are more engaging than disconnected worksheets that address concepts with no context other than completing a worksheet.

You will see a huge difference in your child's view towards learning and accomplishments when they are expected to use higher level thinking skills. But how do you uncover the type of curriculum your child is currently using, and if it is disconnected, how can you shift things to give your child learning experiences that will make them happy and successful?

---◇---

CAUSES & FIXES

Connected curriculum matters to your child's well-being.

So why I have walked through hallway after hallway and seen the same sad look on children's faces, and the same dull texts and workbooks open?

Why are so many teachers teaching content with the lowest two rungs of Bloom's taxonomy — remembering and basic understanding, while ignoring the higher-level rungs — apply, analyze, evaluate and create?

There are some good reasons this type of learning remains so entrenched, and understanding these reasons can help you make it better for your child. You may not like the first reason, and it may not apply to you, but parent expectations about what learning should look like in school holds a lot of sway.

CAUSE 1
LOW EXPECTATIONS

I often have parents tell me, **"My child is bored at school, but school is supposed to be boring, right?"**

When parents tell me this, they look to me with a smile for reassurance that this is supposed to be the case.

And I could not disagree more.

If you teach something with low level thinking skills, it is boring. If you use higher level thinking skills, it becomes engaging.

To see this in action, let's take the most boring thing I can think of teaching: how to take standardized tests.

Here is a disconnected way to teach the language of standardized tests:

Give students worksheets with multiple choice questions similar to standardized tests. Some students get the language. Others don't. But the teacher just keeps giving the students these types of questions, without additional guidance.

Here is a connected way to teach the language of standardized tests:

- After evaluating some multiple choice questions and discussing how they are written, students are assigned to write ten multiple choice questions at the end of each social studies and science unit.

- A peer answers the questions, and also grades the quality of the questions.

- The teacher chooses the best questions from each student for a unit test.

Doing this, students quickly become masters of the multiple-choice test language. They love writing, none of the above, or "a" and "d" but not "c." In addition, students realize, for the first time, that it is actual humans who write standardized tests. They have a whole new confidence when taking standardized tests. This approach involves creating and evaluating, higher level thinking skills, in addition to remembering and understanding basic information.

Next, let's examine another "low expectation" parent mindset.

"My child is bored at school. School is boring, but so is work, so at least they get used to it."

I do 100% agree with part of this statement. Life and work aren't always exciting. And yes, both can be downright boring at times. But I have one caveat. The most fulfilled adults do boring work as a necessary part of something they find interesting. Or they find a way to make to make it interesting, perhaps by improving workflow or systems.

And so, yes, I agree that good curriculum should have its tedious parts.

If you are building a bridge for an engineering challenge after school, you might need to try fifty different ways to make it not collapse. And children will.

In addition, when done in appropriate doses, tedious mindless work can at times provide its own form of relaxation. Sometimes my students were quite excited to do a close ended worksheet after an involved and demanding group project. And close ended multiple-choice tests can be a fast way to see if children have mastered the curriculum that they have learned using more interesting teaching methods.

But this type of purposeful exposure to tedium as a part of a larger goal is quite different from an endless stream of work that feels boring and disconnected in a number of different ways.

The third "low expectation" parent mindset to examine is:

"My child is bored in school, but teachers can't possibly individualize the curriculum for every student."

When I ask parents why they think it would be so difficult to individualize the curriculum, I discover they are usually picturing copying thirty different worksheets for thirty different students, basically creating one-off curriculum for each child. That *would* be difficult to do for each subject.

But you don't need to do that to individualize the curriculum.

There is nothing worse than telling the teacher your child is bored, and having them give harder, but equally boring, worksheets.

There is much excitement about new technology for some very concrete skills, like learning math facts and computation. I believe it holds promise.

However, children from a very young age are very motivated by their peers and social situations. Sitting separately in a room staring at a screen for longer and longer hours has its own set of side effects.

It is very possible to individually challenge each student in a group setting without having one-off work. How?

Designing curriculum that works for a range of individual children is really about opening up the curriculum, and providing choices.

By calling for higher level thinking skills, the curriculum becomes individualized to ability, preferred mode of learning, interests, and social skills.

Let's take an example of how to individualize curriculum comparing learning photosynthesis with disconnected vs. connected curriculum:

My first year teaching, I asked my fourth graders to write a paragraph of the process of photosynthesis, after giving them a presentation of how it worked.

Reading and grading them was so boring. They were all almost the same thing, copied with likely very little idea of what they were talking about. There had to be a better way.

The next year, I approached it differently.

I explained it much the same way, but gave a different assignment to help them integrate and understand the material.

The new assignment was: "Now with a team or working solo, think of a way to really explain to a younger student why photosynthesis is interesting and how it works. As Albert Einstein said, "If you can't explain it to a six-year-old, you don't understand it yourself." You can make a picture book, poster, song, poem, skit, model, etc. Add what questions you are still curious about. You can also do other research if needed to understand it better.

"We will present your idea to your classmates before sharing it with the younger students. And you will be able to improve your presentation based on feedback."

This work was fascinating. So many questions came up as they worked that they needed help understanding. It was both increasing the learning and a better assessment tool. Each child's face was aglow preparing their presentation. Is this curriculum individualized?

Your child can include what they already know about the subject. If they have watched a National Geographic special at home, they can include the interesting things from that show. Your child has to understand it very well, to explain it to a younger child and field questions. Your child is motivated by a real audience to make it interesting. The assignment has no ceiling if you know a lot about the topic. On the other hand, if you don't have any prior knowledge about photosynthesis, you are not overwhelmed. Your child can use a preferred mode of learning, (visual, kinesthetic etc.) to access and cement the material. They are also exposed to other modalities as they hear presentations to gain a deeper understanding. And your child will work in teams on a common goal to use social tendencies as a motivator to learn, and to become more accomplished at teamwork. Or if your child is feeling more introverted that day, they can choose to work solo.

The whole class has the same assignment, but the nature of the assignment makes it individualized.

Your child might still be assessed on photosynthesis with a multiple-choice assessment, since it is an efficient way to assess knowledge, but s/he has learned the curriculum and improved higher-level thinking skills.

Your child can absolutely have engaging, individualized curriculum.

How do you help them get it?

FIX 1
Set Your Expectations

The best way to help your child is to set your expectations for higher level learning.

As you examine your expectations for your child, try to remember what you loved and hated about school. What was a favorite project you remember?

Think of what you truly want for your children. Remember they are in school roughly 1,440 hours through high school. If you loved the way you learned in school, you may want the same for you child. If you didn't, try to make it better for them. Being aware of your experiences will create the freedom to make the best choices for your child, not just the ones that are most familiar to you.

Once you are at least slightly convinced that school can be interesting for your child, you have a head start. But what if you don't really know what they are learning in school or how they are learning it?

CAUSE 2
HAVING NO REAL SENSE OF WHAT
YOUR CHILD IS LEARNING

I hear many parents complain that they have no idea what their child is learning in school. What is the curriculum, for example? What is the approach to learning? Here are some checklist items to help address that issue:

FIX 1
Scan the School

Whether you are looking at a new school or your current school, walk around after drop-off or before pick-up. The doors may be closed to the classroom. That doesn't matter if you can see children's faces through the windows. This is what you can look for without being close to the action:

- Do the children look happy and engaged? If so, that is a good sign. Or, do the children's faces look sad or bored? Not a good sign.

- Are all of the students silent in class and after class? Not a good sign. Silence can be great if children are focused on interesting projects and individual work. But there should be a balance of silent activities and active learning.

- Are the children mainly listening to lectures, reading texts, workbooks, and worksheets when you walk by? Not a good sign. You should see some partner talking, group work, and movement.

- Is the work you see on the walls basically identical? Not a good sign. The very things that look perfect in a class-room can mean that the student just followed mindless directions for a teacher's pre-cut-out activity. Assignments that involve higher level thinking skills will have unique contributions from each child.

FIX 2
Gather Feedback

When the curriculum is strong and the teacher is caring, children are engaged and usually pretty happy about school. They still may not say they like it (it is, after all, school), but they don't generally say they hate it. Are they ever excited about a project at school? If they are not, this is not a good sign.

FIX 3
Do a Rapid Work Sort

Take a stack of your child's work that they bring home, both classwork and homework. Then divide it into two piles.
- Close-ended work that requires only the lowest two levels of thinking: remember and basic understanding.

- Open-ended work that requires higher level thinking skills: apply, analyze, evaluate, and create.

About what percentage of each is your child getting?

FIX 4
Volunteer

If it is possible to volunteer, even once in the year, you will learn a lot.

For example: A class can be silent and no one is really learning or a class can be noisy and no one is really learning. Try to observe the following:
- Has the teacher presented the topic in an interesting way? In 10-15 minutes or less? Research shows most humans cannot attend to lectures longer than that; we tune out. Young learners must be actively engaged.

- Is there a challenge that involves choice, is clearly connected to the goal, and involves higher level thinking skills? Do the students know what they are to accomplish and by when? Is the noise and movement in the classroom mainly connected to this challenge, or are the students just goofing off? (I personally think that social talk is okay in appropriate doses. Most adults interject personal conversations into work meetings as a way to bond.)

- Does the teacher use peers as a way to motivate learning? Are students asked to share and get feedback from peers at some point in the lesson?

FIX 5
Assess the Big Picture

Considering all your "research," check off the boxes in each category. This will give you an idea of what how your child is experiencing the classroom.

General Markers of Connected Curriculum

- All levels of thinking, recall, and understanding: Apply, analyze, evaluate, and create
- Clear goals, whether content or process goals
- Way of teaching clearly matches the goal
- Lively children, sometimes quiet, sometimes talking
- Children are social creatures who also need down time to themselves, the curriculum will reflect a balance of solo and group work
- Choices provided on how to tackle learning
- Work or projects all look different
- You do see your child's thinking or personality in the work
- If your child has mastered content, they are given additional challenges

CAUSE 3
NOT HAPPY WITH YOUR CHILD'S CLASSROOM CURRICULUM

Once you have a sense of your child's classroom learning environment, and you are not happy, you can do the following:

FIX 1
Request Teachers Who Teach with Connected Curriculum

In February of each school year, tell your child's teacher that you really value student learning with higher level thinking skills and 21st century learning. Ask them which teacher is the best fit for that type of learning next year. Teachers have a good sense of other teacher's teaching styles, and can give you a good recommendation.

If your child's current teacher uses disconnected curriculum, they will be less likely to know what you are talking about, or give you a useful recommendation. In that case, ask other parents which teacher uses "hands on learning," or ask the principal. "Hands on learning" is a term that is often used for connected curriculum. Or just look at the next year's classrooms when you walk by. It can become remarkably easy to tell.

Once you have an idea, request the teacher you prefer, saying you feel s/he is a good fit for your child's learning style.

FIX 2

Appreciate

Whenever you notice a higher-level thinking curriculum designed to connect to your child, say thanks to the teacher, and cc: the principal, curriculum directors and anyone else you can think of. Explain how impressed you are and the positive impact you see on your child. By showing gratitude, you are helping to create a culture that supports a higher-level thinking curriculum. Even if a teacher is barely ever teaching this way, they may do it more if they see that parents are noticing their teaching style and appreciating it.

FIX 3

Request Higher Level Work

If you don't see higher level thinking skills in homework, you have some options. You can have a conversation with the teacher and say that you are noticing a lot of the papers coming home that require recall and remembering, but you haven't seen as many papers requiring higher level thinking skills, such as applying, analyzing, evaluating, and creating. As you can't be sure exactly what is going on in the classroom, just say that you wanted to double-check if those types of activities are happening. Perhaps there is no paper trail and the teacher is using dry erase boards. Literature discussions may or may not have a piece of associated paper. And books students write might stay in the classroom for all to read during reading time.

If the teacher seems very open to feedback, you can say that your child responds best to hands-on work and discussions, and your hope for your child is that s/he is exposed to lessons involving higher level thinking skills. Thank the teacher for considering this in future planning. Keep it very friendly, so the teacher is more likely to be open to suggestions.

In addition, it would be useful to meet with the principal, especially if the teacher has been defensive. You can likely point to the school's mission statement and just say you aren't seeing work that relates to that. (Most mission statements speak to these higher-level thinking skills.) You can ask for the principal's support. Stay calm, but be persistent.

Be clear about what you are asking for: work that calls for children to apply, analyze, evaluate and create. Slow and steady wins the race.

Even if you achieve commitment to a connected curriculum for half the time your child is in school, it will make a tremendous difference.

FIX 4
Interview

Ask to review the interview process at your school to learn how teachers are screened.

Then ask to be on the interviewing committee. If you can get on the committee or nominate someone, make sure you or they are asking candidates what they have seen that works or doesn't work in relation to caring and curriculum.

Make sure that teachers teach an active hands-on lesson as part of the interview process to see if they have the skills to teach connected curriculum.

The next cause for disconnected curriculum is related to how society views the purpose of school, and how long it can take to update this purpose as our society changes.

CAUSE 4
OUTDATED VISIONS
OF SCHOOL PURPOSE

There are a few traditions, deeply entrenched in schools in the United States, that are tied to "drill and kill" curriculum.

Schools were designed initially for farmers. Before calculators, to make it worth leaving the farm, performing basic computations for selling crops was important.

The school system in the United States became compulsory for students in the industrial age. Therefore, there was an emphasis on creating factory workers, (hence the bells), focus on following rote directions, and sitting still for set intervals.

Though designed for needs of yesteryear, many schools have retained these influences; education is slow to change.

There are also outdated methods for evaluating teachers.

When I was observed teaching, the administrator would come and sit in the back of the room. S/he made a chart, with boxes for desks, and scanned the room at set intervals, putting x's by the "desks" that were fidgeting, "off topic," or "not quiet."

Close-ended, recall worksheets tend to be solo and silent. Higher level thinking activities, working in teams and doing hands on learning, not so much. This can lead less confident teachers to over-emphasize rote work-sheets for the adults (administrators, other teachers, or parents) walking by, rather than creating learning experiences that are in the best interests of the children. They want to make sure their classroom looks in control, rather than risk the judgment of others.

Adding to the mix, teacher training can accidentally encourage the same curricular methods that they see as ineffective. For example, teachers for credentialing programs may give long lectures about how long lectures are ineffective, without modeling new ways to teach and learn.

Finally, there is another purpose layered on top of the others: to pre-pare students for college. And college learning can be skewed: lecture, take notes, regurgitate the notes you took. And so, the question becomes how will a connected curriculum prepare students for this reality? And though many colleges are challenging themselves to prepare students to solve real problems, these changes take time. Meanwhile, employers are finding that graduates, even those who have done well, are ill-equipped to juggle, adapt, and figure things out in fast- paced work environments. How do you help your child feel engaged in school given these realities?

FIX 1
Shadow a Student

When you observe, volunteer, or talk to your child, try to empathize with the child. What does the set up for the day teach them vs. what do you think they need to succeed in today's world?

FIX 2
Don't Be Impressed with a Silent Classroom

A classroom is not a factory. Be vocal about supporting engaged learning, even if it isn't silent, to free teachers up from the fear of "getting in trouble" for having a noisy class.

FIX 3
Ask the Teacher to Break Up Long Lectures

If you see long lectures, note-taking, and regurgitation, ask if the teacher can break it up with lessons that require higher level thinking and discussions. Even stopping every 10 minutes of the lecture to have students discuss for 3 minutes (what surprised them the most, and what they wonder) can really elevate the learning.

FIX 4
Help Choose Curriculum

Try to get on a curriculum review board of your school. If the curriculum is automated, with rote reading of directions and rote worksheets, advise against adopting, with the argument that this is only addressing low level skills. Try to find one that blends lower level skills with higher level thinking skills.

FIX 5
Set Mental Mindset for College

Students may likely need to take notes for college, and listen to lectures. So, in middle school and high school, students can prepare for that. But encourage teachers to let students compare the effectiveness of notes, and consider what a professor will emphasize when considering what notes to write. They can practice taking notes for different "types" of teachers, those that favor minute detail vs. big picture ideas, for example. In addition, a clever teacher will teach note-taking skills associated with higher level thinking skills, saving space for questions and connections to further thinking.

As always, you want the children to have the practical skills they will need, taught with higher level thinking.

In addition, when you visit colleges, look for the same markers of connected curriculum as you do before college. There are many refreshing models which involve more than regurgitating teacher lectures.

Next, let's examine a crucial piece to disconnected curriculum — disconnected textbooks.

CAUSE 5
DULL TEXTBOOKS

Two quick questions:

1. Do you find your child's text books interesting to read?

Uh, no, because I bet you haven't ever read them. I am an educator, and I haven't. They are too dull. I may have skimmed them to help our son find an answer. But did I sit and read them? No, I did not.

1. Who do you think writes your child's textbooks and workbooks?

Educators? Subject area specialists? In many cases, neither.

In the elementary textbook market, in order to be adopted, all K-8 materials (textbooks + workbooks + teacher supplement books + any related software for each grade) have to be ready for one huge date: the state adoption deadline.

The big three states are New York, California, and Texas. These are the only states that really matter in the high stakes elementary textbook publishing world.

If you get adopted from one of these three, you will have the money to cover the costs of creating the texts, and smaller states will follow suit, leading to more and more adoptions. The smaller states rarely consider series that aren't approved by the big three.

If one of those big three states does not adopt your materials, you have effectively lost all of the time and money that went into developing the materials.

Given the number of years between adoption cycles, it is very difficult to have real experts write K-8 content to this one deadline.

So "authors" write an outline for elementary age texts. These "authors" often have cachet in the field. But they usually just create a scant outline: of topics to cover.

The outline is shipped out to writing houses. The writers at the writing houses are neither educators, nor subject matter experts. They have only a cursory understanding of the subject matter or the minds of the students they are writing for. So, the writing lacks the insight that make a subject matter come to life.

No one means for it to happen, but the way the larger system is set up

FIX 1
Read A Textbook with Your Coffee

One morning in your child's 13 years of school, grab one of your child's textbooks or workbooks and read it while you have your cup of coffee or tea. What is it like to read it?

Later Google the same topic in your favorite newspaper, TED talk or a periodical you like to read.

See what you notice.

FIX 2
Help Select Curriculum

The standards—whether they are state or national—are similar. It is "how" they are taught to children that is important.

Ask your school how much they spend on purchasing texts, related material and professional development for those texts. Could the school/teachers work together to pull from resources to create their own curriculum to meet the standards for far less money?

If that is a no go, which it will probably be — even though good teachers will end up doing it anyway — then try this. Find out how your child's school chooses curriculum, and ask that parents be able to review options. When you review, circle activities that are higher level thinking vs. lower level. Consider how engaged the children will be in learning. Are there discussions, hands on activities that involve student choice and input? Try to engage parents to support adopting these better choices. Texts will often use buzz words that include higher level thinking skills, but look carefully to see if the works actually calls for these skills in a meaningful way.

often leads to lackluster learning materials. So how can you help your child get more interesting learning materials? Here are a few items to try:

The next cause of disconnected curriculum is an over emphasis on test prep.

CAUSE 6
THE IMPACT OF TESTING ON LEARNING

An administrator once shared with me the connection between the curriculum focus and testing.

He explained that test scores are linked to real estate values, so they are enormously important to our parents. The brightest children score well regardless, so the school doesn't pay much attention to them. It can be difficult to raise scores for the lowest scoring students. But for students in the middle, if they can find and identify specific weaknesses that correspond to the test, they can raise their scores significantly. So that is what they focus on. The skills on these tests are often out of context and quite low level, so it skews things in that direction.

I was left with an image of Arnold in *The Terminator* when he sees zeros and ones as he scans a room. Teachers are seeing numbers instead of children when they look around.

Test scores measure things like:

- How to multiply accurately
- How to measure something
- The time frames of the world wars
- Correct grammar and punctuation

Test scores cannot measure:

- Higher level thinking skills
- Creativity
- Real Life Problems
- Perseverance
- Communication skills.

Successful, confident schools can set a goal. Well-educated children can take standardized tests, learn their content, but can also create, persevere and communicate successfully. The leaders at these schools teach to "the whole child." They believe content knowledge and process skills are important for success, and they teach both. But not all schools do.

On top of having testing potentially dumbing down the curriculum, depending on how the school approaches it, if your child's test is norm- referenced, then the test won't even tell you if any particular skills have been learned. Instead, a percentile rank is assigned: how your child performed compared to other children. For example, if your child is in the 51st percentile, they performed better than 51% of the children who took the test.

Do that mean they know a lot, or not so much? You can't really tell. It depends on how much the average child knows.

A bit of history might be helpful. The first standardized test popular in the United States was the SAT, introduced in 1926, for college admissions. For selective admissions, many thought it made sense to see who was in the top 10% compared to others.

However, this style of testing was handed down to elementary schools without much thought.

Criterion-referenced tests are different. They can tell you if your child knows the standards for that grade. They are scored to measure a child's performance compared to an expected standard of mastery. On these tests, your child would get a percentage, say they knew 80% of the material, not

FIX 1
Have a Balanced Approach to Test Scores

When discussing test scores with other parents, keep in mind that standardized tests mainly measure recall and basic understanding, but don't measure higher level thinking skills. Try to keep that distinction in perspective.

During conferences with teachers, do not focus only on the test scores. Instead, blend in discussions about what your child does well, what makes them happy, and deeper goals that you might have.

When parents mistakenly exert intense pressure on their child's school to have the highest test score possible, it can adversely impact the curriculum to become all multiple choice test prep understanding, but not higher level thinking skills.

FIX 2

Determine Type of Standardized Test

Look up the test your child takes and see if it is norm-referenced or criterion-referenced. Here's how to tell quickly. If you get a percentile rank, the test is norm-referenced. If you get a percent score, it is criterion-referenced.

The problem with using norm-referenced tests with elementary students, is that they get re-normed, so that 50% will always be in the 50th percentile. This means you can't be sure if a student knows the standards – how to read or do the math. Maybe most students are performing amazingly well, or quite poorly. You won't really be able to tell. Most admission tests, such as the SAT, are norm-referenced, so eventually, you will have ranking information.

Criterion referenced gives you a better sense if your child learned what was expected of them in that grade.

a percentile ranking.

Given this testing landscape, how can you keep your child's work from becoming all test prep?

Next, is another hidden cause of lackluster curriculum that I discovered at a teaching conference.

CAUSE 7

TEACHERS FEELING THEY SHOULD KNOW IT ALL

Once, at a science teaching conference, the presenter started the discussion by mocking students' and adults' understanding of seasons. He read off explanations that were wrong, each leading to laughter.

But if you listened carefully, the laughter was uncomfortable.

It is difficult to grasp, for any of us, how the sun and planets are spinning around at thousands of miles an hour, and that it is the angle of rotation, and not the shape of the elliptical orbit around the sun, that causes the seasons. It is particularly difficult to understand the seasons when you are looking at static images in a text.

This mockery was a brief moment in the conference. What difference could it make?

I think a great deal. The moment of laughter and humiliation exemplifies an entire approach to teaching and learning.

There are facts. If you get them wrong, you are stupid, and should be laughed at.

Instead of laughing at a common misconception, why not use the misconception as a teaching moment?

Often, the more you *really* try to understand something, the more questions come up and the more you learn.

I propose something different than mockery for teaching a concept.

I have noticed that the more confident the teacher, the more s/he praises excellent questions, the more s/he tries to model tenacious questioning and learning alongside her students, and the more s/he can praise a gifted brilliant child who knows more about a certain subject than she or he does.

The less confident the teacher, the more offended the teacher seems to be by excellent questions and accelerated students. They shut them down, or answer a complex question in a simplistic, inaccurate way. And so much is still unknown:

In physics, dark matter . . .

In biology, how tree roots are communicating with each other...

I once read about scientists spending years trying to figure out why the bubbles in a Guinness beer went down instead of up.

I recently got an email from a former student:

"Thank you for your elementary class. I am Calvin Lau, from all the way back to the fourth/fifth grade class. I can't remember if I e-mailed you when I first started my PhD program five years ago, but I wanted to update you because you are one of the teachers who has specifically influenced my path into the program.

I just successfully defended my thesis for my physics PhD about two weeks ago! I just wanted to thank you because one of the important events that led me into this program was a tiny moment in the class when you were discussing possible curriculum and nuclear fusion was brought up for a brief minute or less.

I still remember you explaining that nuclear fission was splitting atoms and nuclear fusion was combining them, and that either method gave energy, but fusion was better. It was because of that moment that I looked up nuclear fusion when I decided to go into physics in high school, and because of that, I have worked towards nuclear fusion research. Starting from the next year, I will be working for TAE Technologies, a private nuclear fusion energy research company, as a Scientist.

I am very thankful and appreciative of your influence on the path my life has taken!"

I recalled what he was talking about. I literally had spent about a minute on something that had puzzled me as I was preparing to teach the physics lesson. Fission was the power source of nuclear reactor plants. Yet, fusion produces the power of the sun, and you don't hear as much about it as a power source. I wondered why.

That was it. I just shared something that puzzled me.

FIX 1

Support Professional Development

Ask to review the professional development opportunities for teachers at your school.

Instead of giving money generally to the school, try to "adopt" teachers who can both attend professional development related to higher level thinking skills, and then share it with teachers at the school, and provide ongoing support. This will increase teacher confidence in new methods. Without this sharing and follow-up, the professional development will have limited impact on students.

FIX 2
Teach "Not Knowing" at Home

Don't leave one of the most important learning motivators to chance. Teach "not knowing" at home.

Give your children hard challenges that you don't care about—making a ramp for sledding, for example—and encourage them to patiently create solutions. For any hard project, let them flail a bit, even cry . . . and just keep saying, what could you try next? You are building tenacious problem solving and perseverance. If the ramp never works, so be it. They will realize tomorrow that the world didn't end, and next time, they can apply all that didn't work to something that does.

Have your child reflect on why something works or why it does not, so it informs their next move.

You have taught them how to learn.

Don't over-instruct or give too many directions. Let your children figure out how to make a bed, load a dishwasher, or cook. If the results won't be catastrophic, stand back and let them experiment, try different things, and fail. This absolutely means being okay with it looking like a child did it, rather than an adult.

Praise what they figured out or, at least, tried to figure out. Don't take over.

Because their interests are a part of the equation, let them feel important. It is their agenda and goals, not just ours.

Be confident enough to bring up the mystery of unanswered questions. Read, wonder, and talk about what you don't know. Nurture a lot of curiosity in your child. If your child's teacher shuts down this curiosity, explicitly tell them that great discoveries and work are always preceded by questions that others didn't even think to wonder about.

Caring is the essential base layer for your child's best learning environment.

Connected curriculum is the well thought out plan.

There is one final "C" your child needs: **Creative Problem Solving**.

PART III

THE FINAL "C"

—CREATIVE PROBLEM SOLVING—

WHAT I HAVE SEEN

The best laid plans always have to adapt to an actual child, on a certain day, at a certain time. Which means even with caring and connected curriculum, lesson plans rarely work perfectly in the classroom.

Learning may not be happening when it should. Your child's behavior may be perplexing.

I once taught a student who had learning issues associated with having spina bifida. He had an aide read with him once a week. She complained to me that he wasn't retaining anything or making progress. His reading scores weren't budging.

Though they worked together in my classroom, I was typically preoccupied with the other students, so I had never really observed the interaction between the aide and this boy closely. Observing closely in a lively classroom (in this case with 40 4th and 5th graders) is harder than it sounds. Like training waiters who shadow the waiter to really hear a one-on-one conversation, you have to be a few feet away, and the class has to be fairly quiet.

One day, I had the rest of the class do silent reading (an activity that guaranteed mostly quiet), and sat a few feet away to watch how the aide and the student interacted. With the book closed in front of them, the aide asked: "What happened in the last chapter?"

The boy looked scared by this question. It had been a week since they had read together, and he couldn't remember. He was very eager to please, but he just didn't know. The aide opened the book and asked him to read out loud. He read haltingly. It was a bit painful to watch.

After their time was done, I asked her if she always started this way. She said yes.

I told the aide, that I (and many people) are rarely able to "cold remember" a previous chapter of a book a week later. I usually flip through the last chapter before I start the new chapter, in order to jog my memory, especially if a few days have passed.

I also shared how my mind would go blank when my dad would ask me to solve complicated math questions in my head, without pencil and paper. He always looked mildly disappointed at the time it was taking me to figure it out. And over time, I got so anxious that my mind would literally go blank as soon as he asked. I was not only *not* thinking about the math problem, I wasn't able to really think about anything. I was worried this same "anxiety deer in the headlights freeze" was happening with this student. I wondered if anxiety from a question he couldn't answer (for good reason) was shutting this student down in the first few seconds of their interaction, and nothing else could go in.

In addition, I had noticed that if I am reading a book out loud to my class, I retain much less than when I read silently. The skills needed to read aloud well (using different voices for different characters, pausing for cadence and suspense) take away from my comprehension and retention abilities. I can either read well out loud, and not really know what I have read, or read silently and follow it well. And I am a skilled reader, not someone learning.

I wondered if reading aloud was actually impairing this student's reading comprehension skills.

So, I asked the aide if she could experiment with something different for a few weeks, to see if it might help.

I asked *her* to flip through the previous chapter, and recall and comment on what had happened previously. This would be a model for him, and give her empathy for how it feels to remember.

Then I asked her to read out loud *to him* for a few weeks, also to reduce his anxiety. Then they could discuss what happened in a genuine way to work on comprehension. She did.

Next we experimented with having the student skim the previous chapter himself, and discuss it with her.

Finally, we resumed having the student read out loud to her. But we also gave him some time to re-read silently before they discussed what happened and why. That way, he could work on reading fluency and comprehension appropriately.

His reading scores skyrocketed.

Creative problem solving happens with careful observation born of genuine curiosity, rather than judgment or blame. I could have just said, "This student is not capable." Or, "The aide is not doing a good job." Neither of those statements would have led to a solution.

Once, visiting a possible preschool for our son to attend, I watched preschoolers talking non-stop during story time. One preschooler literally just got up in the middle of story time and wandered around the class.

Terrible, right? Rude, right?

If you walked in at that very moment, you would think the class very misbehaved.

But I was sitting and watching the class before the children talked and wandered off.

Here is what happened:

The teacher called all the little preschoolers to the carpet for a story. She had them all get quiet. Then, after all the energy it takes to get preschoolers quiet, the teacher left her chair to go get the story to read. She didn't have it picked out ahead of time, and she stood flipping through several books, deciding which one to read. The preschoolers had now been sitting for a while, with nothing to do, and were antsy. The teacher returned and said she would wait for complete silence to start reading the story. The teacher finally started reading. An adult walked into the class. The teacher stopped reading the story, left her chair and started talking to the adult, for quite some time.

That is when the children started to talk. One boy wandered off from the carpet, while the teacher was talking to the other adult, probably forgetting that it was even story time, since the teacher was not reading.

The teacher returned with the book, yelled at the class for being disrespectful, and in particular, yelled at the boy who wandered away— and in front of the whole class.

I overheard the teacher telling the aide later that she was going to call this boy's parents.

I wasn't there for the call, but the teacher likely said, "Your child got up in the middle of story time and just wandered off."

The parent might have scolded the child, even punished him.

Having watched the scenario unfold, I felt the preschoolers' response was a pretty logical one, given the situation. Had the teacher been prepared, and sat and read a story with an engaging voice, the preschoolers would all listened with rapt attention.

But the teacher was unprepared and unfocused, and the students were left feeling bad about themselves, having no way of understanding what just happened.

I got a call one day that a kindergarten student attending our after-school enrichment classes had tried to kick our teacher. This kindergartener was frequently yelling and screaming that she hated Workshop and the teacher. The teacher didn't know what to do. She had tried to ask the girl what she didn't like, and had gotten nowhere.

Would I call the parents?

I was almost tempted to do so in this situation, as the behavior seemed out of bounds.

Instead, I reminded myself of all the times I thought I knew what was going on, but really did not. I started asking questions.

I knew this teacher to be a caring and creative teacher. We discussed the curriculum for the kindergarten class. I couldn't see any problem over the phone. So, I arranged to visit at a time when this student typically got frustrated.

During the visit, I soon noticed that there was a lot of waiting time before the class even started. The child was as happy as a clam at sign in and during the outdoor break. But the line had to be quite perfect to go inside, and this took a while. Then the children had to sit on a white line, waiting for the others to go to the bathroom, and there was nothing to do. I watched this kindergarten student get antsier and antsier with each wait. I could understand how she felt.

She seemed happy when the teacher read them a book and discussed it, but then the "centers" started. The centers were play-based literary and math activities.

The centers, rather than being true choices, were a forced march. The students had seven minutes at each center, and had to do all of them in a certain order. Quiet was urged. One center was the homework center. The children looked downright depressed heading to this center after a long tiring school day.

When I had encouraged centers in the context of kindergarten students and our after-school classes, I didn't picture set minute rotations. What the kindergarten students loved, in my experience, was being sparked by choices of building, imagination, math and literacy related activities. It worked best when the students had the choice to stay with one the whole time, or move around as desired.

The little girl I had come to observe looked sad. She wasn't ready to transition at certain intervals. She didn't want to do more homework that felt like class work, immediately after school.

After the class, I asked the teacher why she had set it up this way. She said that several of the kindergarten parents had wanted the child's homework to be completed at this time. Because of this, she had to keep the class quiet and make sure everyone rotated through the homework center.

It became clear to me that this kind teacher, in trying to please these parents, had designed a classroom that was not a good fit for most kindergarten students right at the end of the school day. It was particularly not a good fit for this bright energetic, imaginative girl.

I explained to the teacher that I would take the heat with the parents and re-redesign the kindergarten workshop to work for them. I wrote an email to them and explained that this special kindergarten time was to be focused on math, literacy and imagination skills, with choice for the students. If the kindergarten parents wanted the homework completed, the kindergarteners would need to stay for our study skills class later in the afternoon that was designed to meet this goal.

With the homework taken out of the kindergarten class equation, now the students had the same options (minus the homework), but could choose to stay at one center the whole time, or switch as their interests switched. That choice or control (that all humans love) made all the difference.

I asked the teacher to try the class the next day with two small differences – starting class more quickly and providing true choice.

One day after the new, more appropriately designed centers came in, this same girl ran up to the Workshop teacher, hugged her and said, "I love you, and I love Workshop."

The kindergarten students were able to complete homework successfully with the older students at Study Skills Workshop, after they had recharged their batteries.

The devil is truly in these details. Seemingly small routines hold enormous sway in their impact on learning and behavior.

Do students have a little time to connect with each other at the beginning of the day, just as all adults do when they enter a meeting? How would you feel if you walked into a meeting and were shushed the instant you entered the room?

Are quieter activities balanced with more active ones, so children don't have to sit still for too long?

And if there is specialist help for your child, is it scheduled carefully? I was surprised when children were pulled from my class during the very subject they needed help with. Or they were pulled mid-lesson and returned mid-lesson. The students returned lost, with no idea what was going on. Tweaking this experience to make sure the specialist help occurs at a less important curricular time, and is lined up with the beginning and end of class, can take the student from feeling lost, to being successful.

If you don't design a schedule around a child's needs, frustrations build into anger and acting out.

It might be rethinking one sentence, a schedule, or lesson design that makes all the difference. But you won't get to that change without creative problem solving.

WHY IT MATTERS

One year, I happily brought home my students' writing assignments to grade. My mood soon soured.

I had forty 4th and 5th graders that year. I realized that if I just looked at their writing assignments for five minutes, it would take me 200 minutes. That was 3 hours and 20 minutes to look at one assignment!

And having been an editor, I knew that it would take much longer than that just to read the paper, much less give meaningful feedback. Even ten minutes would still be too short to do a useful edit, and that meant 400 minutes, or 6 hours and 40 minutes to look at one assignment.

And there were obviously other assignments to grade. So even working astronomical hours, I would fall short.

In this case, I realized having forty children capable of editing was better than having me be the only one capable of giving feedback. So, I set out to teach the students to be editors as well as writers. They became responsible for meaningful edits. We practiced editing for each part of the rubric. We practiced copyediting. I then reviewed the edit, and agreed or disagreed with their assessment, giving my reasoning. I did follow up copyedits to see if they missed anything. 100% correct equaled an A.

Students tried harder knowing a peer, and then a teacher, would both be giving feedback. They got the feedback they needed. Editing made all the students better writers. I could give useful feedback in a reasonable amount of time.

There are many, many teaching challenges like this to figure out daily.

The first few years of teaching I worked until very late, and every weekend for many hours. Eventually, I was able to fit in time to work out, and time to sleep. But if a teacher cannot solve work/life balance issues, that teacher will burn out quickly.

Behavior management strategies also require creative problem solving.

When I was introducing the lesson, I would often mention the word "partner" or "team." And then the children did just what you would expect any social creature to do. They spent the rest of the time making eye contact or talking to make sure they would get paired or teamed up with their friends.

I learned to make the words team or partner the very last thing I mentioned, and allotted a set amount of time for them to talk and work this out. Or I gave them ways to form groups such as, "Find the three other people with a matching picture."

The teacher considers both his or her goals, and the child's, when designing the day.

I think holding the idea of designing a happy day for students is key, rather than thinking of it only as "managing their behavior."

I made this mental switch myself the year that one of my students had what we thought at the time to be a terminal cancer. I woke every day thinking: *What do I want this day to be like for him?* By considering this one student's day, all the students benefited. And so did I. It was our class's best year. (And I got to see him at a reunion organized years later, and was thrilled.)

A great teacher assumes that children want to be successful and is not afraid to redesign a classroom experience until that happens.

If you have an energetic or imaginative child, this curious problem solving becomes all the more important.

One day, after watching an incredibly energetic student create new outdoor recess games, I put my hand on his shoulder and said, "I love your energy. You are so much fun." He said, "What did you say?" When I repeated it, he looked like he couldn't take it in. I don't think he had heard the words love and energy in the same sentence before.

When I told his mother this story, she burst into tears. Suffice it to say the phone calls from school had described his energy differently.

When teachers can't creatively problem solve, your child will bear the brunt of the rigidity.

Even though sitting still for more than two hours a day is associated with many negative consequences, active children get scolded for not being still, or they are scolded for not keeping hands to themselves. Child play is very touch centered. Touch grounds children.

Imaginative children get scolded for daydreaming, which means they often don't follow directions well. When children are bored, they often slip into imagining as a way of passing the time. Certain teachers can be very threatened by this, without really considering if the child is engaged in learning.

Adults can forget what it feels like to get in trouble, and to be constantly criticized.

Try to recall a time you were even slightly scolded as an adult. I was recently publicly scolded for sitting on the grass in a beautiful garden. I was sitting peacefully writing and hadn't noticed a sign. I was left with a unique mixture of embarrassment and resentment. It is not a good feeling.

From what I have seen, I would guess that active or imaginative children come home having been scolded or corrected more than ten times a day for things that are basically central to their nature.

Often the passive aggressive, or negative comments, are said one-on-one, so even volunteering in the class, unless you are very observant, you might miss what the child is experiencing.

The onslaught of criticism can lead a child to try to shield themselves. Children may become anxious or withdrawn, or try to be less of a target of the criticism by becoming invisible. Or they may become angry. They may say they don't care about the criticisms to protect themselves. The less control the child feels about getting in trouble, the more bravado they can build around it. They may quit trying, and daydream more – anything to shield or soothe themselves.

The same criticisms can spill from school to home, changing the child's home experience as well.

These criticisms often come in the form of what I like to call a "magic wand phone call."

Calls home *can be* collaborative, with the teacher trying to figure out what is going on with a child in order to use the information to make the school day work better.

Calls from school *can* be like this, but often they are not.

In a "magic wand phone call," the teacher shares something that is going on at school, and you, the parent, are asked to talk to your child to fix it.

I would get calls from our teachers asking me to make these phone calls to parents using our after-school workshops.

"Could you talk to your child about listening better, or . . ."

However, when I would observe the child in the classroom situation that was presenting difficulties, almost all the time, I could see why the child's traits were leading to frustrations. The majority of the time, it was details in the way the learning was set up, not the child, that needed to be shifted.

Some teachers can have a hard time seeing the relationship between the way the environment is designed, and the child's reaction to it.

In my years in education, here are the types of things I have seen that lead children to act out:

• Teachers that really don't like the students and it shows.
• Teachers who say unkind things to embarrass children in front of the class. (In this case, the child might start acting out to gain respect back from their peers.)
• Overly controlling teachers, who focus all their attention on scores of instructions that must be followed to a 'T,' rather than letting the students have some control and choice in projects.
• Children being asked to sit and listen to long lectures – where only the teacher's thoughts matter.
• Boring, uninspired lessons.

Sometimes a "magic wand, please fix your child conversation" happens at pick up with all the other parents watching. The pressure on parents is enormous. Now they feel embarrassed! So, let's consider the parents for a moment. What if they have limited understanding of the problem as the teacher describes it, or they do understand, but cannot fix it because it is not their job to design the learning environment at school.

Now, hypothetically, let's say that a child is very energetic, and the teacher has not built in time to move, have discussions, or other pedagogy to incorporate energy into the day. The child is criticized and scolded in school numerous times for not being able to sit still. Then the parent gets a phone call about the child not sitting still. "Could you speak to your child about this?"

The parent wants to train the child so he or she won't get in trouble at school. So quite possibly the home — where the child could easily be more energetic with no criticism — can become filled with anxiety and scolding to try to train the child to be more still. And this is done to protect the child. The result might be that both environments become inhospitable to natural child energy and the child suffers.

Let's say there is a call home about disrespectful behavior. If the parent starts verbally pounding the child about the behavior, without ever understanding what the child is frustrated about at school, then the child's frustration increases at home as well as at school, with more acting out.

If all parents hear are complaints from the school, they may start criticizing the child as well, for the same perfectly natural child behaviors, thinking they will make the situation better and their child more "successful in school." But really, it is a double whammy. The child has no escape from feeling badly at school and at home.

When creative problem solving is going on at school, you are not as likely to get magic wand phone calls. Here's why:

First, your child's teacher will have mentally rehearsed and refined as much as possible ahead of time, to anticipate and prevent pitfalls. With this mental rehearsal, the teacher is scanning the "invisible curriculum."

For example, consider the task of lining up the students after recess. Children will often not have the self-control to quit playing until after balls are collected. Anticipating this, a good teacher will have sent out ball collectors to sweep balls a minute before calling the class in.

The first way, the students are not listening to the call to line up.

The second way, designing for children's natures, they line up rather quickly.

By anticipating how children work, your child's teacher designs a much better experience.

Let's say the teacher thought through the lesson and potential pitfalls, but your child is still spinning in circles and talking during the teacher's instructions.

There are a couple of choices:

Your child's teacher is upset and asks you to talk to your child about not spinning during mini lessons.

Or your teacher can genuinely start wondering, "Why is the child doing this?"

The teacher can start by asking your child what they think and feel during the mini-lesson. Sometimes children can tell you what is wrong. Often, they cannot. They don't yet understand their psychology, or it is too complicated. So, you have to guess. If the solution improves things, it indicates that maybe your theory was correct. So, a good teacher starts forming some theories about why this might be happening, and considers possible solutions, given each theory. I call this "What, Why, Try."

Creative Problem Solving - What, Why, Try

What: Child is spinning in the back of class during the lesson introduction. This behavior typically happens mainly when students are sitting on the rug and lessons are being introduced. Once the child undertakes a project, it is less of an issue.

Possible Reasons Why	Try
Wants Attention	Ask a day ahead, "Would you like to be my helper for the mini-lesson tomorrow?" You can ask them to write key words on the board, etc. This is nice, because turning your back to students to write, is not a great idea for keeping their attention.
Disinterested	Look at how to grab attention for a mini-lesson. Is it engaging? Relevant? Can you think of better way to pull students in? Are you keeping it to 5-10 minutes, or going on and on?
Don't Transition Well	Have you been very explicit talking them through the transition? I would like you to come in, set backpack on desk, come to carpet, hands in lap, eyes up, repeating expectations.
Hungry	Ask to bring snack to carpet, will occupy them
Get sensory overload	Maybe let them hang back a bit, to have a break
Embarrassed	Are you asking to do things that are comfortable for them? Sometimes I have included a 3-minute partner discussion in a lesson, and the child simply doesn't know how to go about finding a partner, so they act out from embarrassment. Help with that, so it feels okay.
Tired	Say, "You look so tired. Do you want to relax for a while today, until you have more energy?" They will appreciate your caring.
Has extra energy or anxiety to burn off	Test if they are actually listening while spinning. Some children can. If the rest of the class isn't derailed by this, let it go.

To see if the theory is correct, the teacher experiments with related solutions. If it works, great.

If it does not, it could be the theory is correct, but your solution isn't quite the right one.

In other cases, a solution doesn't work because you haven't yet identified the real cause of the problem.

It is trial and error of rapid order, a fast-paced version of the scientific method or design thinking, from theory to testing, in a matter of minutes or days.

So, when you don't get the upset call that your child is squiggling on the carpet, it is because the teacher has done this work. That is the first bonus. Here is another way creative problem solving helps your child:

A teacher who models this type of problem solving allows your child to see how to solve complicated problems.

Whenever I am teaching and don't have a solution, I involve the class. One challenge might be, "It is taking really long to line up from recess, so I have to stop recess earlier to start class on time. How can we line up faster to have more recess time?"

We brainstorm why it might be taking so long to line up, then brainstorm solutions for each issue.

The students become aware that complex problems need multi-pronged solutions.

Having a ball collector helped, but so did timing how long it took them to line up, and having that time gap dictate when I called line up the next day. It was a built-in incentive each day to line up faster; they got to play for longer the next day.

Mastering this more complex problem solving may be the most important thing your child ever learns how to do.

School, poorly done, is a weak facsimile of life. The inches measured in a math text are almost always perfectly to the quarter, or half inch, one-inch mark. Outside of school, I have never measured anything that measures to the perfect quarter, half inch, or inch mark. In school, I studied, I got A's, end of story. I thought real life would be similar.

It was not.

From getting a job, to figuring out a career that meshed with having a child, I had to make it up, carve my own path, and rarely was it clear exactly what I should do.

Students require experience solving real problems with no set answers.

Creative problem solvers show children the inner workings of this important skill daily.

So creative problem solving serves three purposes for your child:

- It means the teacher is happy, and feels optimistic about solving problems.
- It means clever problem solving on behalf of your child, so you don't get magic wand phone calls.
- It teaches your child how to approach the complicated problems they will need to solve.

How does creative problem solving get overlooked at school, and what can you do to make it better?

CAUSES AND FIXES

So, what if the creative problem solving piece is missing? Why might it not be there, and what can you try to help? Let's start with a common, but rather invisible, obstacle to creative problem solving.

CAUSE 1
THINKING YOU UNDERSTAND THE UNDERLYING PROBLEM WHEN YOU DON'T

Creative problem solving requires patience, both patience to understand the problem and patience to actually experiment with different ideas until we figure out a way to make it better.

I have always felt it was the most fundamental part of my job to try to problem solve on behalf of my students. Not all teachers see this ongoing detective work as a part of the job. They feel, "This is the way I do things, take it or leave it."

"I seek to understand and then be understood," advised Dr. Stephen Covey, author of *The Seven Habits of Highly Effective People.*

For some, the "seek to understand" part can get skipped.

When we are impatient, and something is not going the way we want it to, we blame - someone else. We don't try to figure out what they are thinking, and consider our role in how things are playing out.

Too often when things aren't going how a teacher wants, the ego flares. The teacher takes the situation as an affront.

Swift judgment can make us feel assured, but is the opposite of understanding.

To be an excellent educator, one of the most important questions to ask is "why?" Why are we teaching what we are teaching? Why are children doing what they are doing?

This is often not in our nature. We are rushing around. We short cut. We are upset. A child is upset. We think we know why, without giving it much thought. We react based on the story we create about what is going on, without really knowing.

Asking "why" isn't so hard. The hard part is being humble enough to ask **genuinely,** or to ask when your emotions or the child's emotions are bewildering and frustrating.

When our son was in preschool, he came out dressed head to toe in every piece of superhero clothing he could find. I asked why he was wearing this "super-superhero" outfit. He explained that he had seen a bug, and the bug would be scared of him wearing this.

Knowing this, I would handle the ensuing struggles differently. (Because as you can imagine, he would want to wear this super-superhero outfit on many occasions.) Had I not asked, he wouldn't have told me, and we could have had many battles, without any understanding of what was at stake for him.

Asking why is not limited to the behavior of those around us. It is also approaching our own motivations honestly. What triggers us to have intense emotions? Why? What messages or situations have we encountered in life that might contribute to our reaction to things?

Connected to this impatience to create an easy narrative, is a desire for simplicity where it doesn't exist.

What looks like one problem often has many different *and* disparate causes. Each sub-problem must be addressed, often by different solutions. Each solution can impact the other solution. It takes a master problem solver to make progress.

However, rather than tackling the myriad of causes to a problem, we often spin our wheels arguing about what is the one "true" cause of the problem. The teacher blames the parent, or the teacher blames the previous year's teacher. And so on.

For almost any issue, there can be endless arguments about whether the cause is this or that. As if there is only one cause, and it means the other cause can't exist. The time spent arguing about the cause of the problem could perhaps be better spent testing solutions to see if they have an impact.

We also need patience because the first, second, or third idea to fix a problem may not work, and probably won't.

The beginning parts of solutions are full of optimism. You launch something . . . you have a plan, maybe a marble jar for good behavior to get a class party . . . woo-hoo!

But what most people think of as the end of problem solving is almost always the beginning of it.

And if the teacher is not patient enough to tweak, a promising solution can become a dud for your child.

I know a teacher who had carefully constructed a progress chart for a student. Unfortunately, the child would not come meet with her about the chart.

Instead of taking it as a personal affront, she calmly asked the child why he kept missing the appointment to discuss the chart. He said he was worried his peers might see him. To solve that, she put the same chart online, and the child could see and reflect on progress without peers seeing. It made all the difference. Often it is not the whole solution that needs to be tossed out, but only part of the solution needs to be refined.

Large scale education solutions also struggle with this lack of perseverance.

Technology additions in the school can be splashy on the front end, with little support for fine tuning on the back end.

In one district, the teachers received numerous iPads for the students. However, in order to do more complex projects, the students needed to return to previous projects. And yet, the district had put no thought into having children save and return to projects. They said it wasn't possible. Therefore, what the children could do on the iPads shifted from meaningful long term creations to "one and done" projects, often using the same recall and regurgitation of close-ended worksheets.

It was fine they hadn't thought this through. It happens. But in not attending to the reality of what this meant, and in not trying to find a solution, the children were short changed.

A poor mantra is, "I came up with a solution, therefore it is solved."

Maybe you have tried a solution, and don't feel like trying another. You want to feel it is working, so you decide it is.

True problem solvers put most of the energy into the problem right where others drift off.

Creative problem solving requires humility. Why? Because you have to be willing to be wrong on the way to getting it right.

Effective solution building requires a strong "lack of ego" to not become so invested in the brilliance of your solution. If it is not working the way you intended, go back to the drawing board.

Things that worked with one class one year will inevitably not work with the next class. It is not the class's fault. It is just the way things are.

For example, my Writer's Workshop classes always ended with "Featured Authors." It is a tried and true staple, giving children a real audience for their writing. Except one year, it wasn't working, when a group of younger students rushed to write one-page books, just to be designated a Featured Author. I guessed what was causing the rush, and gave the younger students a quick circle share to talk briefly about what they had accomplished that day. This bit of sharing was enough to encourage them to work on longer books to become a real Featured Author.

This is why I find teaching so endlessly fascinating; the process always leads to new surprises and new learning situations.

Here are some ways to enhance creative problem solving for your child in school, even with the innate propensity for humans to skip over thoroughly analyzing the causes for the problem.

FIX 1
Search for "Creative Problem Solver" Teachers

When talking to your child's current teacher, ask which of next year's teachers would be most successful in figuring out strategies that will succeed with your child. Try to request that "creative problem solving" teacher by February.

FIX 2
Share Insights

As soon as possible in the year, preferably by phone or in person, in a 5-10 minute time frame, concisely share anything the teacher should know about your child to best help him or her succeed. If you have seen previous strategies work or not work, at home or at school, share them. How does your child learn best? Share social preferences also. Have your notes ready so you don't take up too much time.

FIX 3
Problem at School? Calls Home?
Keep a Problem Solving Mentality

A great teacher will use creative problem solving to figure out how to connect with your child through learning.

Not all teachers do this, however. Or there can be a large mismatch between what school settings demand and your child's personality. For some, an issue at school automatically leads to a call home.

A call from the school usually spikes anxiety, either from worry that your child is hurt or worry that your child is in trouble.

Your first goal is to calm your own anxiety, so that you can still problem solve for your child.

Strong anxiety is different from worry, in that it is more free form, more overwhelming, and felt more intensely in the body. It isn't "oh, this is a concern, and we'll figure it out." It veers more towards panic.

Anxiety with no idea of what to actually try is "bad anxiety," as you don't have anything productive to do with it. You can and will be angry, concerned, etc. but try to avoid the unproductive free form anxiety.

Unless you have learned strategies to calm this anxiety, it will persist until the child comes home from school and flood out onto the child.

Anxiety is contagious. When you are anxious, your child becomes anxious. Then your child may become more defensive about the situation to try to make your anxiety go away, rather than reflective about the situation. So, the heightened anxiety, in a sense, shuts the child down, and gets you no closer to a solution.

Even if your child has been hurt by someone else, you still need to calm your anxiety. I have seen instances when older children do not tell anyone about important hurtful events. When we press them to find out why, they say, "Because my parents will freak out." It scares children to see parents "freaking out" and they would rather avoid it. But then you are not hearing what you need to hear.

So, when a call from school comes, calm yourself as you would calm a child. Tell yourself everything will be okay, calls from school happen, and breathe. The tried and true technique of taking three deep breaths is surprisingly effective, as it tells your brain you are not in danger and reduces cortisol. Or use any relaxation strategies that work for you. Often just telling yourself that everything will be all right is enough.

You do have to genuinely calm yourself, though. You can't just choose the perfect words to say to your child and think that can cover up anxiety. If you think you can fake being calm, you can't.

You could have two absolutely identical transcripts of a parent speaking to a child, and if you just read them on paper, you wouldn't be able to tell which parent was anxious. But if you are in the room, you would immediately know. Anxiety, like caring, is felt. And children are finely wired to feel it.

One of the biggest fears that a call can elicit is that your child is not normal or okay. As a teacher who has worked with hundreds of children, I can say that children have a WIDE range of behaviors at different times of their lives. Your child won't be the first or last to do x, y and z.

So, try to calm yourself at the beginning of the call from school.

Then what?

FIX 4
Try To Understand the Issue

When a problem comes up, try to find out as much as you can about the problem before devising solutions.

The first goal is to learn more than you knew before.

If you hear, "Can you talk to your child about x?"

Say, I will certainly talk to my child, but I want to learn more from you. Here are a few examples of questions to ask to learn more:

- Tell me more about it.
  - Can you tell me more about when it happens/ happened?

- What happens/happened right before?
- What do you think might be causing the behavior?
- Does it happen in some classes, but not others?
- With some teachers, and not others?

If something doesn't make sense to you, ask specifically more about it.

A wise teacher will have insights.

Then say something like, "Let me see if I can learn more from my child about how to make the situation better. I'll check back so we can come up with a plan to try."

This phrasing leaves the responsibility for trying to figure out a solution resting with <u>both</u> of you. You won't hang up feeling like you need to be a magician and fix things perfectly by yourself.

Without this phrasing, if you hang up the phone with the problem resting on your shoulders, you may feel anxious as well as angry. The child will shut down and you will be no nearer to a solution.

Thank the school, but wait to give your opinion, or agree to a plan, until you learn more.

FIX 5
Talk to Your Child

This will be the hard part to handle productively.

Your instinct might be to say: "Your teacher called. What you did (or said) is totally inappropriate." A good yell or immediate punishment might make you feel more in control, but in reality, you will be less in control, because you might be acting with blind spots in your vision.

You could be missing a great deal about your child and what is going on in school. You could be missing a chance to really help your child, or the teacher.

You can reflect calmly after you understand the situation better.

Remember, if you really want to learn more, try to avoid stress or anxiety when you ask. Your child will be able to be more reflective, rather than defensive, if you can ask in a calmer way. Try to avoid or rephrase yes/no questions.

Open ended questions are better:

- Tell me about . . .

- What is going on with . . .

- How are you feeling about . . .?

- Why do you think the situation is happening?

- What do you think would make it better?

If it makes sense in the situation, always try to acknowledge the child's feelings. For example, say, "You seem frustrated. Let's try to figure out why."

Sometimes just noticing a child's feelings and supporting why a child seems angry, makes them feel less angry.

After talking to your child, see if they have ideas about what is causing the issue, and what would make it better.

FIX 6
Observe Firsthand

If at all possible, and your child is of an age that they are okay with it, say that you would like to come volunteer or observe, during the time the situation is occurring, to help understand the situation. Nothing beats seeing the situation to really understand it better. As you observe, shadow your child through observation in order to gain empathy.

We had one young student who was running wild, and grabbing everything in the after school classes. Stepping back a bit to consider when this happened, we noticed that he did this only when we were moved into the multipurpose room, a large space, due to a conflict with using our regular classroom. When we stayed in our classroom, he did fine. Any classroom change threw him, as it did other students that really needed consistency. We didn't have a lot of control over our classroom space, but we did understand his behavior better.

If a child is fine up until a certain point in the afternoon, sometimes they are just exhausted. Introverted children have to expend a lot of energy on social interactions; they really need down time.

Figuring out what your child needs to thrive is the important thing, not whether the behavior is good or bad.

Take some time to think about what the teacher has shared, what your child has shared, and what you observe.

Once you have a better understanding of what is causing the problem, you are ready to start solving it.

FIX 7
What/Why/Try

After talking to the teacher, your child, and hopefully visiting the classroom during the time the issue is occurring, you can use this framework to start tackling the problem:

1. What is generally going on? Be as specific as you can.

2. Write down any theories you can think of for why it is happening.

3. Brainstorm ideas of what to try for each of these theories.

Start with your thoughts, and then run them past your child and teacher to see if they agree, or want to add anything. Revise as needed.

Consider what seems like the best thing to experiment with first to make the problem better.

Choose one or two ideas to start with.

Now the tricky thing here is that many of your theories for what is causing the problem may involve a mismatch between your child's personality and the classroom design. The solution is going to have to address both. You want to frame this for your child and the teacher.

Let's consider what are typically the top three teacher complaints:

- Child doesn't follow directions well
- Child talks too much
- Child is too active
- Child gets too angry

How can you frame the issue and the solutions in the most productive way?

FIX 8
Following Directions

Let's say the teacher is saying your child cannot follow directions, and when you visit, you notice the teacher gives many complicated verbal directions. This is not your child's strong suit.

To your child, you could say something like:

"Some people have a harder time following direction than others. Your teacher gives a lot of detailed directions for assignments. This is her way, but not all teachers will be this way. Maybe you can jot notes, draw a picture while she talks, or just glance over to confirm you are on the correct step. But it may always be hard for you, and that is okay. There are other things that are easier for you, like being creative, that may be hard for other children." For the teacher, you could say something like:

"I know you are frustrated that Jo has a hard time following directions. Is there any way you could try writing them on the board, or handing them out?

We will practice multi-step verbal instructions at home as well to help build up this skill."

FIX 9
Talks Too Much

To child: "You are a very talkative child, with an inquisitive mind. That will be a really good thing in life, but can be harder in school. There are times that talking can help you learn, and other times when you need to listen in order to learn. I will talk to your teacher about adding more times when you can talk in order to learn. And then I want you to picture an ear while she is explaining things, to remind yourself to just listen. If you have a question, you can raise your hand to ask it."

To the teacher: "Jack is very talkative, and learns by talking. He could benefit from talking to make learning connections. Could discussion questions and team projects possibly be added to the lessons? Then we can stress that he does not talk when you are explaining what you all will be doing next. Maybe you can say, "listening time" for the next x minutes to signal him."

FIX 10
Too Active

To child: "You have a lot of energy, and this will serve you well in life. It can be hard in some schools. I will try to work with your teacher to think of more times you can use your energy. We will pick sometimes when it is really important to try to be more still for you to work on that skill too."

To teacher: "Our child has a lot of physical energy. Can we go through the schedule to think of when movement can take place as a part of learning, so that the energy can be an asset, rather than a liability? And what are a few times daily when being still is the most important to you? We can set those as goals to focus on, since being still all day long is going to be too much."

FIX 11
Too Angry

To child: "Working with others and not getting our way can be hard. Notice as soon as you are getting angry. Ask the person why they are doing or saying that. Say what you want. Try to come up with a new plan that you both like. We can practice this at home when I make you mad."

To teacher: "My child needs help handling strong emotions. This is what I am practicing at home. Could you do a brief lesson with the class on this, so the students are trying the same thing. Or maybe have a corner with a little poster of this (my child could help make it), so students can go there when they are mad to try it?"

FIX 12
Test and Refine

Make sure you have a plan with the teacher and your child to check in to see what solutions are working, what is not, and determine what you might try next, based on what you are noticing. Remember that many times you just need to refine the current solution to make it work. Other times, you may need to go back to your "what, why, try" to devise a whole new solution.

These problems are challenging. Experiment quickly (consider how much time it would really take to see if a solution is working), and then try something else.

Some might say, "Who has time for this?"

It can seem like this attention to problem solving is a one-off. However, when I have designed for what seems to be one-offs, the entire class design improves for all of my students.

This constant challenge can be as interesting as making a discovery in science and uses the same basic mechanism to learn.

The theories of what cause behaviors often clump together to build an invaluable core of knowledge.

On the parent side, dealing with an issue that isn't solved takes time and energy, but so does ignoring the issue. If you understand more about the nature of the problem, you are helping your child understand themselves better.

Finally, though I put the steps out in detail, in reality, they can happen quickly. Learn of a problem at school? Learn more from the teacher, your child, observe. Come up with your leading theory of the cause of the issue. Experiment with a solution. Keep trying until you figure it out.

For some, this problem solving for individual students might make them feel like students are "precious snowflakes," an insult I have heard, but every child is unique and has different strengths and challenges.

Often, a child simply needs to have consistent rules, and understand consequences. This is almost always the first place to consider when "hot spots" arise.

A successful school is not a factory. You can't cookie cutter, stamp, and produce happy children and successful adults. You can't code them to do what you want.

So, if they are snowflakes, you don't want to smoosh them. A teacher's job is to bring out the best potential in every child.

The dialogue between expectations and needs is a two way street. It is not giving the child exactly what they want, and ignoring the needs of the teacher or other students. It is a more intelligent way to design the classroom so all children thrive. It involves an appropriate ego on the part of the teacher. They know a lot. They have expectations, but they also have empathy to consider what the student is needing.

Education is a magical interchange between teacher, classroom and child.

Rather than be annoyed by it, successful teachers are fascinated by it.

FIX 13
Plan A Better School Meeting

Sometimes the problem leads to more than a call home, and the school will suggest a larger meeting. If there is a disability that needs to be accommodated, it is called an IEP (**I**ndividualized **E**ducation **P**lan).

Theoretically, this is the mother lode of creative problem solving for your child. But if you want to make it so, there may be a few pitfalls you will need to avoid.

In private and public schools where I have taught, the concept for the meetings sounded great, with a number of stakeholders weighing in. However, when I attended these meetings, a few things really surprised me.

First, I was surprised that I, the child's homeroom teacher, had never met many of the teaching staff attending the IEP. They had often spent little to no actual time with my student, due to the enormous caseloads they had. Some were only at our entire school for 1-2 days a week. It seemed to me that they were there to check off boxes, and to fill out paperwork to meet legislative requirements. But they did not have much insight into the child we were discussing. This was the case even in a small private school; specialists we hadn't interacted with were suddenly all around the table.

The specialists always spoke a great deal at the meetings. Their vocabulary was specialized, meaning you would only understand it if you were in that area of special education. I knew what the words meant, having been schooled in them in my master's program. I would not have known what they meant otherwise, and most parents did not.

I looked at the parents' stricken faces, trying to take everything in. Hearing that your child is having challenges is stressful. Having seven teachers/counselors/special education specialists all talking to you about your child with inaccessible verbiage is incredibly overwhelming, even more so to the parents who don't speak English as a first language.

The parents often seemed speechless when dialogue is needed most.

The problem or diagnosis was often oversimplified (ADHD and Sensory Processing Disorder were commonly used for a wide range of unique behaviors). But the solutions to help the child feel happy and successful—practical, real life, useful solutions—were hard to come by.

As the child's teacher, I kept asking: What should I try to do to help? I already had some ideas, but since the special education resource was sitting there, I wanted to gather more ideas. The response was often more large vocabulary words.

Both classroom teachers and parents were left unsure what to actually **do** to try to solve the problem. The large words drifted to the ground in the wake of the meeting. The words spoken weren't actionable, meaning they weren't practical to-do's that a teacher or parent could leave with.

If parents feel anxiety from a phone call, these large meetings can lead to overwhelming anxiety at home. Here's how to make the meetings more productive.

FIX 14
Get Key Players

Here's how to make large meetings more productive for your child's needs:

You might want to have a more productive meeting by having only staff there that really know your child, and consulting with the others as needed.

Find out well in advance who has been invited to the meeting. If you want to see if the specialists slated to attend the meeting really know your child, just ask your child, "What do you think of X? What do you all do?" If they barely know who the person is, you may just want to use them as a resource later.

Respond to the meeting planner. Explain that your child has not really interacted with X, and you would like a smaller meeting, and can connect with that resources specialist later as needed.

FIX 15
Find Your Leader

In these meetings, look for someone who might serve as a lead advocate for your child going forward. Look for those that seem to have the most empathy, compassion, wisdom, common sense, and resilience to tackle problems. Whoever it is, try to follow up with them.

If the specialist tries to understand the particular problem at hand, rather than trying to force it into a preconceived box or a certain category, that is a good sign. If you can understand their ideas to try to make it better, that is a great start. And if the person seems willing to keep refining a solution with patience (to figure out why the solution may not be working in its current state), that is also a good sign.

FIX 16
Make Sure You Understand

If you don't understand what is being said at the meeting, ask, ask, ask. If you don't understand the new ideas to try to help your child, ask more about the proposed solution.

FIX 17
Leave with Concrete Ideas

Try to leave with one to three things to try at home and at school. "Actionable" means losing the complicated terms, and really thinking through real life solutions. Contribute your own ideas. Try to follow up with teachers and evaluate solutions. Having an ally to achieve a goal helps.

Don't expect the school to have all the answers. Equally, the school shouldn't expect you to have all the answers. You are united in trying to get at the root cause of any issues to help your child in order to design better solutions.

FIX 18
Note The Tone

If you notice an intense lack of interest in problem solving regarding your child, and an extreme focus on the negative with no positive, the meeting might not be about helping your child, but about building a case for expelling them.

In one of my teaching jobs at a private school, I was called in to the principal to talk about a student. I responded by sharing her strengths, her incredible verbal abilities, public speaking talents, and her determination to tackle math challenges by working with me in her free time.

The principal glossed over these and kept bringing up the child's weaknesses. The child did have struggles with subtracting and division, but her desire to work on these was impressive. The principal kept pressing for more weaknesses, and then asked if I would come to a parent meeting, and only share information about the child's weaknesses.

I did not want to do that, and the principal was quite angry with me about it. She said the child was not a good fit for their school, and that she needed too much help. I could point to other students getting much more specialist help than this student. It didn't matter. The principal said I was patient, but other teachers would be less so.

The school found other teachers and specialists to do what they wanted. They met with the parents and made the case for her "not returning" and "it not being a good fit."

When the girl found out what was happening, she would often sit in the back of the class and cry.

The school expelled another student that year. She had lost her grandparents who were paying her tuition. The parents offered to cover the tuition, but the school did not relent. She too cried in the back of my class.

I begged and pleaded for them not to put the students through this intense rejection, to no avail.

As a result, I switched to teaching at another school. I wanted to help students, not watch a school chop off what they perceived to be weak branches.

If you noticed this level of negativity, this is not a healthy environment for a child or parent.

Another cause for lack of creative problem solving is a tremendous gap in how we teach "experimenting."

CAUSE 2
LACK OF A METHOD FOR TACKLING THE UNKNOWN

In school and in teacher training programs, most teachers are not taught how to approach the unknown. That is a problem for them and the students they teach.

To approach the unknown, you need to become comfortable with experimenting.

However, many schools have a different approach.

To learn to experiment, they teach students to:

replicate an already designed experiment (in which they hopefully have thought through and controlled all the variables)

follow every step perfectly, and get the right answer.

Once you do this for 12 years, in college, or maybe graduate school, you might get to design your first experiment.

I remember my first time well. Towards the end of my Master in Teaching program, I was sitting in my "learning to teach science class." Professor Dick Rezba handed us a bag filled with wires, batteries, and lights. He said, "Experiment. I will check back in 10 minutes to learn what you discover."

Huh? We sat at first. What are we supposed to do exactly? Rezba was silent, looking at us. He said no more.

So, we started experimenting. We touched wires, got a lightbulb to light.

"Hey, does yours do this too?

"I wonder if it is because . . . let me try this to see . . ."

In moments, we were experimenting, forming theories, and testing them.

I wrote in my notebook, "Sixteen years of schooling and this is the first time I have been allowed to truly experiment."

Why would it take 16 years and 10,400 hours of schooling?

Even when given the task of conducting original research, there can be a fear of the unknown. I discovered this when asked to conduct "real" research for my Master's thesis in order to graduate.

I had one question that I had been considering for a while. I was curious if we should be so quick to forbid students from writing about any type of violence in schools.

Many children we were teaching were experiencing violence on a daily basis in real life, not just in movies. I wondered, what would happen if they wrote about what they were experiencing. I thought it would be interesting to allow it in one class, to see what happened. Writing can be a cathartic way to process experiences, and maybe that would be the case here. I really wasn't sure.

I pitched this idea to my thesis advisor. Take two classrooms, forbid it (the norm) in one, and don't forbid children to write about violence in the other, or loosen up the rules somewhat. Watch what happens. I wasn't quite sure what to look for, but I thought differences could lead to further questions.

Her response was that I shouldn't pick this question for my thesis. Why not?

Because I didn't know how it would turn out.

Wasn't that the whole point?

She didn't think so, and resisted approving this research idea, suggesting others like, "Does reading with young children help them become better readers?"

She ended up approving, "Do mediation programs improve environments in schools?" I had been very involved in a peer mediation program in my high school, and had seen first-hand the positive impact. She felt safer about how that one would turn out.

Education academics want to help students learn to conduct research, but they also want to be "right," and they want their students to be "right." Successful academics have been rewarded for being right all along. This focus on being right creates teachers who come to believe that being right is more important than being curious. It makes the research obvious, redundant, and less than useful. It sets a tone for how you approach learning. Can you comfortably attack a problem that you don't yet know the answer to? For every simple or robust accomplishment: how to start a lesson quickly, how to make the iPhone, how to land a rover on Mars, there are many disastrous moments along the way.

Children (and adults) read and hear about successes, without hearing the background stories of challenging spots along the way. Individuals often want to spin their stories to show themselves in the best light possible. This is understandable, but it leaves children unaware of how much effort is required to solve a problem.

FIX 1
Ask the School to Teach How to Experiment

How can you create a curious, experimenting mindset in your child if schools don't always support it?

Ask your teacher, principal or the education board, when are students learning to actually design original experiments? When they point to examples, ask yourself, are they designing, or following directions from someone else who has designed it? If they are designing original experiments, they are starting with a question, and then they figure out how to try to find the answer.

FIX 2
Teach Creative Experimenting at Home

Talk out loud about ongoing setbacks or large problems that you have put a good deal of effort into figuring out, even if you are not there yet.

Tell them the fifteen things you tried to fix the TV. Model remaining calm, figuring out what is causing the problem, and then trying one next thing. They will copy your problem solving ways, and learn to tackle the unknown.

FIX 3
Make Experimenting as Part of Daily Life

Create experiments with your child. Let's take the most basic experiment: a race between two children.

After children race to a certain outcome, ask: was it fair? (Usually you don't even have to ask.)

You will instantly hear things like:

- She had better shoes.
- She started first.
- You didn't watch the end carefully enough.

Challenge the children: How can we make the race more fair? What shoes should you each wear to make it fairer? How can we make sure one person doesn't start first? How can we make sure we know who crosses the finish line first for sure?

Children will be motivated to figure these things out. Shoes, unfair starts, finish line viewer inconclusiveness, are all variables. All you really want to measure is which child is faster. Once you control the variables, you can be more sure that you are just comparing the children's speeds.

Or let's take breakfast. Serving waffles? Have two syrups in the fridge. Tell the kids you are doing a taste test to find out their favorite syrup.

Set up the test. Have them close their eyes to taste each one and rate it.

Ask them after: was that a fair test? If they don't know what you are talking about, prompt them:

- Should I have let your rinse your mouth out after each one in case the taste of the first affected the taste of the second?
- Did it matter which one you tasted first?
- Should I have repeated it more than once to be sure?
- Were you affected by what rating you heard others give?

Come up with a better way to taste test the syrup to solve for each of these problems, and see if the results are the same. Try it on another day and see if the results are the same.

Make children as fluent in designing experiments as they are in learning to read. It is a natural ability, and I would argue as important for learning and growing as reading, writing and arithmetic.

FIX 4
Critique Experiments

Critique what you read out loud with your children. Let's say you read that carrots make you live longer. How did they find this out? How did they rule out all of the other things that could make you live longer? How many people did they study?

Modeling this for your children/students will help them ask the educated questions about research in order to determine whether its conclusions are closer to the truth or less close to the truth.

FIX 5
Laud Truly Creative Research

When you read research or experiments that started with a genuine question, encourage it, applaud it, share it with other adults, and share it with your children.

WE ARE ALMOST AT THE END OF EDUCATING
YOURSELF TO BEST EDUCATE YOUR CHILD.

⸺⸺◇⸺⸺

LETS TAKE A MOMENT TO LOOK AT THE BIG
PICTURE, AND THE QUICK TAKEAWAY.

PART IV

PUTTING IT
ALL TOGETHER

AT-A-GLANCE
BEST EDUCATION 101

When things go wrong for your child in school, when there is lack of caring, connected curriculum, and creative problem solving, there is one over-riding cause. I would call it systemic narcissism. What it means is this: adults are making decisions for what serves them best, not for what serves children best.

If it is missing at your child's school, caring, connected curriculum and creative problem solving needs to be put back into the equation.

We have delved into the many why's of what can lead to a lackluster education for your child, and how to hurdle each one. Here is a quick "at-a-glance" summary of how to get the best possible education for your child, given the very real constraints in many schools.

PROTECT YOUR CHILD AHEAD OF TIME

Before, during and after any experience in school with friends or teachers, make sure your child knows that you love them unconditionally.

Say to your child frequently, "I love you the most. I couldn't love you more, I couldn't love you less. Ever."

Your child will almost certainly encounter different messages from teachers or peers at some point in school. You are the most important person to them. If they are secure in your love, when others are unkind to them, it won't take root as strongly.

RESPECT YOUR INNER VOICE

Everyone has an inner dialogue with themselves. That dialogue can be words we heard as children, usually anything we were made to feel ashamed about, as that has a way of sticking.

When you make a mistake, your inner voice may berate you or reassure you.

Your child will know your voice. You will either share your internal kindness and criticisms directly with them or they will sense them.

Since your inner voice will have a tremendous impact on your child, you should be aware of what that voice is saying, and perhaps make some shifts if possible.

Here is a nine minute quick personal reset. At the risk of embarrassing myself, I've included my own answers to these questions:

Set your timer for three minutes, and write for three minutes to each of these prompts.

What are critical thoughts you have about yourself or others? Where did you get this message? Do you agree with it? Why or why not?

This one feels really personal, and almost all are items I was criticized for when I was quite young. My mom said I was vain for looking in the mirror when I was little, so now I am embarrassed to look in the mirror in public restrooms, even when I probably should. Looking back, almost everyone wants to look good or is curious what they look like, so my mom should not have made fun of me for looking in the mirror. I can feel I am lazy for doing nothing, and this is also from lots of prompting growing up to do something, and not just sit around and read. But being lazy can be recharging your resources and a form of meditation, and without it, you can spin out of control, so I would rather encourage that in myself and others at times, and give it a more positive name. I can say, glad you got to chill today, for example.

What are you kind to yourself about? Where did you get this message?

My mom used to laugh and tease me for how disorganized I was leaving the house and how little time management I had to actually allow enough time to get places. So even though I am still terrible at this, I look at it with amusement, rather than beat myself up. I can be absent minded as well, typically because I wrap myself up in thought about something else rather than daily tasks. My father was like this, and got a lot of good natured teasing about it, so I take it easy on myself about this as well.

Notice your thoughts, and continue adding to the reset exercise. Build your confident, yet realistic voice, so you can nurture your child's.

What messages, positive and negative, did you hear about yourself and others in school?

What are some of your vivid memories of school?

What did you hear said?

What was punished? Do you agree with how things were handled? What would you say now if talking to the person about the issue?

What would you like your child to hear about the same issues?

Here is my free-writing answers:

My elementary school could be brutal to children who couldn't sit perfectly still. As a result, my first times playing teacher, I would write all of the children's names on the board who would get demerits and take some pleasure in this. My school was also quite mean to those who read slower, because there was a projector that put lines up at a different pace, and you were placed in a group by how fast you could read the lines. The children in the slowest group got made fun of. There was a lot of yelling and reprimanding. I lived in a knotted fear that I would do something wrong and get punished. I forgot to write my name on my paper in 1st grade, and my punishment was to go in at recess and write my name the whole time. I threw up before school that day I was so stressed, but didn't tell my mom why, as I thought what I had done was so terrible. I would say now that this was ridiculous and not a very nice way to treat a first grader for forgetting something.

After you have examined a few of your "forming" experiences, the next most important step, if you have not already, is choosing a school.

CHOOSING A SCHOOL

School is often the single most deciding factor (and the most overlooked) standing between a happy, engaged child, and a sad, withdrawn and angry child.

It matters.

Look for a school where you feel accepted and comfortable; your children are likely to feel the same. Note if you feel genuine kindness from those you encounter at the school. Trust your intuition greatly here.

Look for a school where the children seem engaged, happy, energetic, and act like children typically act. A silent, still group of kindergarteners for a long period of time is not the natural order of things. Look for curriculum where at least half of the projects displayed are unique. This tells you which percentage of the projects are connected curriculum vs. simply following a set of complicated lengthy instructions. How would you describe the culture of the school? Robotic or experimental?

ALREADY SETTLED AT A SCHOOL

If your child is in school, and you aren't sure a search for a new school is in order, you can still work to make it the best experience possible.

First, talk around and think ahead to request the teacher that you feel has the three C's most in place, explaining why these qualities will be a great fit for your child. Get requests in first, as it is easier to accommodate than if your request is one of the last received.

Remember that the same teachers who are annoyed at requests, almost always make requests for their own children, for one simple reason: the quality of the teacher has an enormous impact on almost every aspect of your child's life that year.

When you walk around the school and in your child's class, try to get an overall sense of the level of caring, connected curriculum and creative problem solving in play.

Start and have an ongoing conversation with your child about the three C's (but you don't need to label it as such). I know it is tiring, but talking time before bed can be a golden time (when they may not want to sleep, so are lured to talk). To learn about caring, you can start these discussions. What is your teacher like? Why? What is an example? What did they say? Tell me more. Be calm and inquisitive, so they don't shut down. Share stories from your school life, to get the conversations going.

For connected curriculum, look at the level of thinking your child's assignments require.

For creative problem solving, consider how problems are handled. Are you and the teacher a team trying to figure out why a behavior is occurring, and brainstorming things to try in class and at home to make the situation better?

If you see examples of the three C's strongly in place, verbalize for your child why you think it is great in specifics. Write an email, and say thanks for what you appreciate: cc'ing every possible person you can – curriculum director, dean, vice principal, principal etc. Describe for the school what a positive impact that the three C's has on your child.

If you see one or more or all of the three C's missing, start a conversation (at whichever level makes the most sense – teacher, curriculum coordinator, PTO etc.) Adapt the relevant message(s) into your words. Try to be tactful and calm. And follow up. Did the ideas work, why or why not, and what can we try next?

MISSING CARING

Frame it for your child. Empathize.

For example, you might say to your child:

I think you may not be liking school, because your teacher is not being very caring. It is normal for students to make mistakes, and it is something to work on, but it doesn't mean there should be yelling or . . . If I were getting yelled at during the day, I would feel pretty stressed out and not great. Explain the strengths you see in your child. Explain how that will serve your child through life, while also presenting challenges in certain settings.

Discuss it with the most appropriate persons at school, given the situation:

Elevate the conversation if you are not seeing a difference at all.

You might say something like this to the school:

My child responds well when s/he feels the teacher likes him, and understands his or her strengths, in addition to goals for improvement. The following situation has made my child feel like the teacher doesn't like him. What are your thoughts on this? (Seek first to understand and then be understood.) I know you care about all children, or you wouldn't be a teacher. Can you help flip the script here for my child, and consider some ways to help him feel appreciated, to understand his strengths, and have an appropriate number of easy to understand goals?

MISSING CONNECTED CURRICULUM

Frame it for your child. Empathize. You want your child to understand why they are having the type of reaction they are having:

I think you might not be liking school because the curriculum is kind of simple – just these worksheets, and they seem kind of boring. I would likely be bored, too.

Discuss it with the most appropriate persons at school given the situation:

I am looking at the work from the past time period, and a lot of it is falling into the lower level of thinking skills, rather than the higher levels. What are your thoughts on this? (Seek first to understand and then be understood.) I think it is really important that the students be challenged in their thinking. What can we do to include a wider range of thinking challenges?

If there are opportunities at any level for a curriculum change, try to review the curriculum and search for and support connected curriculum.

MISSING CREATIVE PROBLEM SOLVING

When a problem arises at school, ask the teacher if you can work together to brainstorm specific reasons why the problem is occurring. Ask your child, too.

Visit the class during the time period when the problem typically occurs to gain more insight.

Pick the most likely reasons for the problem. Just for those, come up with ideas to try (at home and school) to make it better. Don't give up if the first three or fifteen ideas don't work, and don't be afraid to try multiple possible solutions at the same time.

Most problems don't just have one cause, and therefore don't just have one solution. Get the child's input on how it is going, even if the solution seems to be failing. *It doesn't seem to be working. Why do you think that is?* Sometimes it isn't scrapping a solution entirely, it is tweaking it.

Parent: Our star chart to help you complete your homework doesn't seem to be working. Why do you think that is?

Child: Well, I have to get fifty stars for a big reward and that seems like it will take forever.

Parent: What do you think might work better?

Child: Maybe five stars for a smaller reward?

Parent: What do you think the smaller reward should be? (Negotiate, sharing your reasoning, but make sure some of their ideas are included.)

This patient tweaking is where workable solutions are designed.

FRUSTRATED BY LACK OF IMPROVEMENT AT SCHOOL

Your family's school lacks some or all of the Three C's, your child is not happy and hates school, and your efforts to make things better are not getting anywhere

Make sure to frame for your child **why** this setting may be difficult for them. Pull in the context of the 3 C's as useful to help them understand. This helps them understand the situation could be temporary, and the connection between environment and their reaction.

Try to find things outside of school—either for fun at home, enrichment classes, interactive museums, documentaries—that present learning with the three C's. This will keep an ember of a "like of learning" in there, and help your child experience how they feel and respond to a different setting.

Beg for the most "three C" teacher the following year. Explain that your child is shutting down, miserable, or whatever you are seeing.

If the child is hearing a ton of negative comments at school, either about academic abilities or just your child's traits like high energy, or a struggle to follow complicated directions, counterbalance this by really looking for positives at home.

For example, perhaps you can help them have positive interactions for homework. Even if they don't need help, it can help your child become connected to someone who sees the positive in him or her (and is connected to learning). An older child from the neighborhood can be great. Tell them the teacher is really hard on the child, and the goal is to get to know your child and be positive. This can help build a more solid inner voice for your child.

Look at other schools to educate yourself about possibilities and consider how your child's traits would fare in different settings. It can be eye opening and liberating mentally to see what else is out there. If you feel you can't make the change, it is still valuable to let your child visit another school that you think might be a better fit. They can see how different learning settings can be and how they feel in a different setting. If just for one day. Just tell them you think it is beneficial to see how different people do things.

Keep searching. New schools open all the time, and sometimes you will learn about a great option that you didn't know existed. Ask about scholarships. If you decide not to make the move (usually the hardest part is leaving friends), you are still showing your child there are options.

Consider home schooling. In many areas, it is a more social and networked experience than in the past.

Take it seriously if a child really seems to hate going to school. It could be issues we discussed here, or issues with peers. It is the hugest part of your child's life. Say you are sorry. Hug them. Try to help them understand why they hate it. Try things to fix each particular issue. Don't give up. If you don't succeed, your child will feel cared for since you are trying.

No school is perfect, but the closer the school is to having the Three C's, the happier and more successful your child will be.

Even if your child is older, and you look back, and your child's whole school experience was less than you wanted it to be, at least your child had an ally along the way, supporting them and helping them understand why they might feel the way they do. Your child had someone who taught them to keep trying to make things better. Many successful adults can point to this support as a lifesaver in an unhappy school situation.

In addition to the solutions suggested in this book, I hope that parents incorporate a framework for tackling the unique challenges facing their families regarding their child's education

Your child has a journey at school, and you have one as well.

FINDING YOUR VOICE

The journey of securing a strong education for your child can be an arduous one.

I started my parenting journey knowing clearly almost exactly (from my own years as a teacher) what I wanted for my child's education, and in what circumstances he would feel most happy and successful.

Though I knew what he needed, at various times, and for long stretches of time, I completely failed at securing them for him during the school day. At first, I felt, "I won't be one of those annoying parents (and even worse, a fellow teacher) asking for specific things for my child. It will all be fine." I soon realized this was creating lasting confusion for my child.

One night, I watched our son cry for hours. That day, his teacher had ripped up a paper dramatically and thrown it in the trash, because it had no name. She said she would find out whose paper it was. Our son was hysterical, fearing the paper was his. It turned out not to be his, but that was really beside the point. I tried to explain this to the teacher — how afraid he was — and she said, "Good, I want them to be afraid."

On another occasion, he looked so sad when he came home from school. His teacher had asked the children to come up with equations that equaled two. His equation had multiplication, which he had learned when I had tried to entertain him in the grocery cart by letting him press 2+ over and over on my phone. He would try it with 2+, then 3+, 4+ and so forth.

Because his equation included multiplication, his teacher said, "Try not to be so clever," in front of the class.

This time, I tried to speak up, but the teacher said she wanted the simplest equations. She said they were safer. I was at a loss for words to try to explain why I thought this a shallow approach, and a horrible way to make a child feel. In addition, the equation was correct. It was just class work, not a test, but still, he felt terrible.

I didn't say anything after she said that, as I didn't know what to say, and didn't want to make her mad at me and then take her feelings out on my child.

At this point, I realized that I had to at least help my son make sense of this, even if it meant deviating from always backing the teacher. I explained to him that his creative equation was correct, and that there were literally infinite correct equations that equal two when you thought about it. I tried to give him a different perspective than what the teacher was giving him.

Another year, I failed completely, when missing the impact of the teacher who was screaming, ripping up papers, and saying things like, "Can't you ever do anything right?" I watched our son physically wilt, and his self-esteem plummet. Years later, our son would often repeat out loud much of what the teacher yelled at him during that year. It had become a negative internal voice that I was desperate to remove.

Realizing that I had missed this was torture for me.

The teacher part of me planned, researched and wrote the parts of this book that go behind the scenes in education, because it is fascinating to look deeper.

But I think the parent part of me wrote this book out of a sort of penance, so that other parents don't blindly walk down some of the paths that I walked down.

During the years after this really awful year, I watched our son shine under a teacher who gave him the basics for a good education. He was on fire. He loved the teacher, and he loved the subject for years after.

I watched him literally flatten under teachers who lacked the three C's, even more so as it reminded him of the terrible experience early on.

And over the years, I slowly gained a voice, to be able to communicate to our son what he needed and to talk to teachers about what would help him the most.

One year, within a few weeks, I got two phone calls from two different teachers.

The first call was to say how engaged our son was in his class, and how insightful his comments were. I thought there would be a "but," but that was it. He had just called to let me know that. I thanked the teacher. I had heard stories from our son, and saw projects which demonstrated that this teacher was caring, had connected curriculum, which included tons of discussions, and had crafted his classroom setting to respond to realities of educating teenagers.

Within a few weeks, a different teacher called to complain that our son made too many comments in class, and "Could I talk to him about this?" I asked if our son was raising his hand. The teacher said he was, but it was still distracting from his lecture. It turned out the teacher was lecturing for the whole 90 minute block, without facilitating comments or discussions.

What could I say? One teacher valued discussion as part of learning, and the other did not. I could say that discussions help our son process what he is learning, and that he is more successful in a classroom where student discussions are a valued part of the curriculum.

I could talk to our son about both experiences, and why one teacher viewed him as a rock star (for his comments) while another was annoyed (by the very same types of comments). The second teacher only valued his own thoughts during the long lecture, rather than being interested in the thoughts of students as well. Rather than be baffled or damaged by the complaint, our son could clearly see his strengths and goal—to read teachers and try to adapt.

Most importantly, because I could see our son's strengths in relation to the Three C's, the second call created less anxiety that it would have before.

In the past, I am sorry to say, I would have exuded this "you did something wrong" anxiety to our son, trying to be the good mother and back the teacher, fumbling around telling him to not share comments in this class, or who knows what I would have said.

But the takeaway of this anxiety for our son would have been: "I did something wrong, something bad, but I am not sure what. So, there must be something wrong with me."

And that, more than anything, is what I want your child NOT to feel.

Even if everything about your child's personality runs counter to what a school demands, I want them NOT to feel that.

Let's say your particular child is super active, doesn't process or follow directions well, is day dreamy, questions everything, and simply doesn't listen well at all.

There is nothing wrong with your child. The fit between them and an education without the Three C's just might be horrible. But your child isn't. Even on the 8th call from school, complaining about the above, your child still isn't horrible.

Gaining a voice on behalf of my child with my child's teachers was a complete 180 degrees from how I was raised. Here is the internal dialogue that my childhood created:

- Don't cause trouble.
- Don't be one of those parents.
- Always back the teacher.
- Smile and nod at teacher conferences (and doctor appointments).
- Above all, be agreeable.
- Your child can deal.
- Your child has to get used to different "styles."
- This will prepare them for life.
- It will all be fine.

And yes, your child will definitely need to get used to different teaching styles. There is no way around it. But if one of the styles is shaming a child for being a child, or shaming them for trying to challenge themselves by doing work at a higher level of thinking, then your parent voice needs to be stronger.

Your child needs to hear your parent voice, in addition to the teacher's voice, to help them as they create their own fledgling inner voice — that inner voice that becomes the measure of their worth — that inner voice that matters more than any external success or accomplishment.

I started as a teacher who believed wholly in other teachers. And then I began to see that this blind trust was mistakenly placed at times. Now I trust other teachers who give children what they need to learn.

I continue to be intimidated sometimes. *Oh, here goes the annoying teacher telling me how to teach*, I think. That inner voice is still there.

Or, I worry that speaking up might make the day worse for my child. Because at the end of the day, I am not with him in the classroom, and don't have real control over what the teacher does.

My mentor, the former director of the Bay Area Writing Project, said speaking up on her daughter's behalf about the writing instruction was one of the most difficult things she had to do. She was very intimidated, even though she was an expert.

For these reasons, the attempt at improving education for your child can seem overwhelming.

I began my college application with the line: "You can't do everything, but you can do something."

And it is very true. Because when I have the inner voice telling me not to speak up, I have another voice that I have cultivated with great reflection that tells me *to* speak up, that it is the right thing to do. Children are pretty helpless *without our help*.

Because education is so important and impactful in your child's life, I hope that you will take the time to do *what you can*.

If nothing else, I hope you can see more clearly what your child might need, and jiggle and wiggle and urge things towards that. If nothing else, having your child know what would make a better education will help them. Helping them understand their normal reactions (boredom, frustration, daydreaming) when it falls short, will help them.

This knowledge will change how they see themselves and what they search for in life.

When I read bios or talk to friends, almost all of these same "active day dreamy non-obedient as children now amazing adults" had someone in their lives who supported them and provided calm guidance even when, or especially when, schools did not.

Imagine if Einstein's mother had sided with the teacher who said he was stupid.

These kinds of children aren't the easiest to teach or parent. They aren't super docile and obedient. And so? When you are an adult, being obedient only goes so far. Questioning goes a lot further. So does lots of energy.

If you are the parent of a child who doesn't fit in well to the heel print of school, you will be called on to do more. You will need to understand your child's reaction in relationship to the success or failure at the three C's. You will also need to weather the perception of other parents.

I was a child who did not listen well. At home, I climbed on the roof and to the edge, over and over, despite repeated punishments. I recall once, wanting to use an axe to chop a branch off a tree that we were trying to cut down, just like I watched my older brothers doing. My mom said, unequivocally, no, I was too young to wield the axe. And so, I waited until her attention was elsewhere, and tried to axe one of the branches. A few axe hacks in, the axe slipped on the milky sap in the tree, and gashed me right under my knee. Blood squirted everywhere. My mom was furious and concerned. She bandaged it and propped my knee up on pillows to slow the bleeding. I sat in bed and thought and thought about that branch that wasn't completely chopped off yet.

I snuck out of bed, tiptoed across the house, went outside, got the axe and tried it again. Within a few strokes, the axe slipped again, and I gashed my other knee—even worse than the previous gash. I was bleeding profusely again and terrified of the anger that would ensue. I was bandaged again.

I sat in bed again. And thought and thought and thought about that branch that wasn't completely chopped off yet. I couldn't quit thinking about finishing that project until it was complete. Eventually, I finished it.

From my mother's perspective, this must have been frustrating. I was disobedient. From my perspective, I didn't intend to be disobedient, I didn't want my mother to be mad at me, nor did I want to be punished. But I really, really wanted to do take care of that branch, and the satisfaction of proving I could do it made the punishments and bloody knees worth it.

I have tons of other stories like this when, after setting my mind to do something, I decided to face the consequences rather than be deterred.

And, now, in retrospect, I realize these disobediences were absolutely critical to my happiness.

As a teacher, I always did what was best for the children. I didn't use the curriculum I was supposed to, if it wasn't working for my students. And I kept designing experimenter's workshop, which led to an award winning article and to the start of my company, despite the disapproval of my principal.

In my axe story, and in my childhood, there are two things of note in my mom's reaction. I learned that disobedience has consequences and I learned that I had to decide if I was willing to risk getting those consequences.

But my mother never shamed me for the disobedience. She was annoyed and angry, but not shaming. It was kind of like this. You are a child. Of course you are going to want to do these things, like climb onto the roof. And of course I need to punish you.

Another parent might have said, "What is wrong with you?" and shamed me for my disobedience. My mother understood that I was in pursuit of a vision, even one as silly as cutting the branch off with an axe like my brothers had done. Often, I would overhear my mom saying to others, with some measure of pride, how stubborn I could be. I saw this character trait as something potentially good in me.

Stubborn. Taking risks. Persistent. That's who I was on that tree and who I still am today. When I had only one student registered on the first day of my after school enrichment classes, I gulped and decided to take it as a challenge.

And if I had to point to the exact one thing that more than any other has helped me lead a life I am happy with — it is this exact thing. Once I set my mind to something, I will persist, even more so when it becomes more difficult.

This was one of the traits that my mom appreciated and encouraged. Your child will have different ones.

I invite you to consider the incredible gift you give when you help your child understand their traits, and know when traits will be an asset, and when they will present challenges.

I invite YOU to do this for your child, not to wait for the school to do it for you. Because the school might leave your child more focused on weaknesses than strengths.

Please do not be too hard on yourself. Doing everything in this book will not make your child's education perfect, by any stretch. But it will make it better, if only in the building of your child's identity. And even if that is all you accomplish, it could be the difference between a happy and successful life for your child vs. an anxiety filled, stunted one.

For the systems in play — public schools, private schools, unions, testing companies, publishers, colleges — change is rare and difficult. Keep chipping away at it. It is a goal worth exerting effort for. And if parents are asking for meaningful things for their children, it just might start to budge.

Best wishes and hugs on your journey of education with your child. You will both always be learning, and trying to do the best you can. And that's the best any educated parent can do.

I will add that I was unexpectedly diagnosed with stage 4 colon and liver cancer as I was doing final edits on this book. So, I send it out in the world, not quite knowing what my state will be as it moves forward. But if one more child comes home from school smiling, because a parent understands what their child needs to smile at school, then my spirit will be smiling too.

CONNECTED CURRICULUM IN ACTION

ACKNOWLEDGMENTS

I WOULD LIKE TO THANK:

My Dad for writing a book when I was a young girl, and showing me it was possible.

My Mom for starting so many sentences with, "I wonder…"

My high school for showing me a better way of learning, which inspired me to go into education.

Dick Rezba, my college education professor, for asking me to design my first experiment, and teaching us how to educate students without hours of lectures.

Carol Tateishi and the Bay Area Writing Project for encouraging the same teaching strategies that my principal nixed, and for always encouraging me to ask "why"? I will always remember my initial interview with Carol. She spoke very little, but asked "Why do you think that worked?" and "Why do you think that didn't work?" Forming these theories improved my teaching dramatically.

My fellow teachers, Taryn LaRaja, Jen Bloom, and Wendy Osborne for being that welcoming place to go after school, and inspiring me with their talent and dedication to their students.

Susie Cresci for being the most integral part of Workshop Education since day one, and always being the wise, creative problem solver that she is.

Joanne Knaus, for being willing to mull over the details with great insight to figure out why things are working or not for our Workshop Education students.

All of the teachers at Workshop Education over the years who have demonstrated caring, connected curriculum, and creative problem solving beyond what I could have imagined. It has been a delight to walk into classrooms to see the resulting smiles on so many students' faces. You have shown me daily how much the three C's really matter.

All of the students through the years, for teaching me how to see the world with new eyes.

Lana Guernsey, for her searching and inquisitive nature, and for saying to me that she felt I had something to share about education.

The first readers of this manuscript for their incredible, helpful encouragement and feedback: Rick Frisbie, Taryn LaRaja, Lynne Ruppel, Leslie Samuels, and Alexa Dahl.

My husband, Rick Frisbie, who has been relentlessly positive and supportive of my education endeavors since we were 18 years old.

My lovely friends who have gathered around me to help me know that even with cancer, I am never ever alone, and putting a spring in my step to complete this book.

The whole team at Mediacs publishing for their ongoing enthusiasm and understanding completing this project with a lot to juggle. Their kindness and belief in the project have meant the world to me.

For all the parents and educators that will add their stories, ideas, and strategies for improving education for children, and carry on this work.

I feel truly blessed for the support leading to this book. My love and appreciation to all who have touched the lives of student's in such positive ways.

ABOUT THE AUTHOR

Since graduating from the University of Virginia with a Master's Degree in Teaching, Alexa Stuart Frisbie has taught in San Francisco's public and private schools, trained teachers, created award-winning curriculum for NASA and UC Berkeley's Bay Area Writing Project, and published articles on exemplary practices in teaching writing, math and science in various publications including *Learning Magazine, The National Writing Project* and *Curry Magazine.*

In 2009, Alexa founded Workshop Education, an after-school program of enrichment classes recognized by the *Bay Area Parent* magazine as a Family Favorite for Educational Support. Workshop Education has served thousands of students. *Secrets of Your Child's Education* draws from these experiences to give parents the tools they need to crate positive learning experiences for children.

Made in the USA
Middletown, DE
14 January 2021